Education Wins

Modern Learning and Teaching

Daniel Dennis

ISBN: 978-1-77961-986-0
Imprint: Telephasic Workshop

Contents

Introduction

Purpose of the Book

Providing a comprehensive overview of successful educational practices

In this section, we will explore the importance of providing a comprehensive overview of successful educational practices. When discussing education, it is essential to highlight and analyze the strategies and techniques that have proven to be effective in fostering positive learning outcomes. This comprehensive overview allows educators and learners to understand the factors that contribute to educational success and incorporate them into their own practices. It also serves as a guide to inform decisions on curriculum development, classroom management, and instructional design.

To begin, let us define what we mean by "successful educational practices." These practices refer to the approaches and techniques that have consistently shown positive results in improving student learning, motivation, and engagement. They encompass a wide range of teaching and learning strategies, including personalized learning, project-based learning, flipped classrooms, differentiated instruction, and technology integration, among others.

The first step in providing a comprehensive overview of successful educational practices is to analyze and synthesize existing research. Various studies and research papers have explored different aspects of education and identified techniques that have yielded positive outcomes. By examining this body of research, we can identify common themes, principles, and strategies that contribute to educational success.

One common theme that emerges from the research is the importance of personalized learning. Personalized learning recognizes that every student is unique and has distinct learning needs, preferences, and strengths. By tailoring instruction to meet these individual needs, educators can promote deeper understanding, engagement, and motivation. Strategies such as adaptive learning technologies, individualized learning plans, and formative assessment are integral components of personalized learning.

Another effective practice is project-based learning, which emphasizes hands-on, inquiry-based approaches to learning. By engaging students in real-world projects and problems, they develop critical thinking, problem-solving, collaboration, and communication skills. Project-based learning provides students with opportunities to apply their knowledge and skills to authentic tasks, enhancing their understanding and retention of concepts.

Flipped classrooms have also gained popularity as an effective educational practice. In a flipped classroom, students engage with instructional content outside of class, typically through online videos or readings, and classroom time is dedicated to collaborative activities, discussions, and problem-solving. This approach maximizes face-to-face interaction with teachers and peers, promotes active learning, and allows for individualized support and feedback.

Additionally, differentiated instruction is crucial for addressing the diverse needs of students in the classroom. By modifying instruction, assessments, and learning materials to meet individual students' levels, interests, and learning styles, educators can create inclusive and engaging learning environments. Differentiation fosters student success by ensuring that all learners have equitable access to educational opportunities.

Lastly, technology integration has become a significant factor in successful educational practices. Technology offers various tools and platforms that can enhance teaching and learning, such as interactive simulations, virtual reality, and online collaboration tools. When used effectively, technology can engage students, facilitate personalized learning, and provide access to a wealth of resources and information.

In conclusion, providing a comprehensive overview of successful educational practices is instrumental in informing and guiding educators and learners. By examining research, understanding key principles, and exploring specific strategies, educators can adapt and enhance their instructional practices to promote student success. This overview serves as a valuable resource for professional development, curriculum design, and innovation in education. By embracing effective educational practices, we can create a more engaging, inclusive, and impactful learning environment for all students.

Key Principles: - Personalized learning recognizes and responds to the unique needs of each student. - Project-based learning promotes hands-on, inquiry-based approaches to learning. - Flipped classrooms maximize face-to-face interaction and promote active learning. - Differentiated instruction addresses diverse student needs and learning styles. - Technology integration enhances teaching and learning experiences.

Challenges and Potential Solutions: - Implementing personalized learning can be challenging due to resource constraints and time limitations. Schools can plan and invest in necessary technology and professional development for teachers. - Project-based learning requires careful planning and alignment with curriculum standards. Teachers can collaborate with peers and share best practices to ensure effective implementation. - Flipped classrooms may face resistance from students who are not accustomed to independent learning. Educators can provide clear guidelines and scaffolding to support students in their independent learning journey. - Differentiating instruction may pose challenges in managing classrooms with diverse student needs. Teachers can utilize formative assessment tools to gather data and inform instruction. - Integrating technology effectively requires a thoughtful selection of tools, training for educators, and considerations for equitable access. Collaboration and ongoing professional development can address these challenges.

Example: An example of a successful educational practice is the implementation of personalized learning in an elementary school. The school recognized that students have different learning needs and abilities, and a one-size-fits-all approach was not sufficient. Teachers incorporated personalized learning techniques by incorporating adaptive online learning platforms, conducting regular formative assessments, and providing individualized support and feedback. As a result, students became more engaged, achieved better academic outcomes, and demonstrated increased confidence in their abilities.

Resources: - "Personalized Learning: A Guide for Engaging Students with Technology" by Peggy Grant and Dale Basye - "Project-Based Learning: Real-World Examples of Success" by Suzie Boss - "Flipped Learning: Gateway to Student Engagement" by Jonathan Bergmann and Aaron Sams - "The Differentiated Classroom: Responding to the Needs of All Learners" by Carol Ann Tomlinson - "Technology Integration in the Classroom: Tools for Effective Teaching and Learning" by Elizabeth Sky-McIlvain

Tricks and Caveats: - It is crucial to understand the needs and interests of students when implementing personalized learning techniques. Building relationships and rapport with students can help tailor instruction effectively. - While project-based learning promotes student engagement, it requires careful scaffolding and clear guidelines to ensure that students stay on task and achieve the intended learning outcomes. - Flipping the classroom requires thoughtful planning and consideration of students' access to technology outside of school. Providing alternative resources for students without internet access is essential. -

Differentiating instruction requires ongoing assessment and data analysis to ensure that students are making progress and receiving the support they need. - When integrating technology, it is important to consider privacy and ethical considerations related to student data and online safety.

Exercises: 1. Reflect on your own learning experiences. Identify a moment when personalized learning made a significant impact on your understanding and engagement with a subject. Share this experience with a colleague or discuss it in an online forum. 2. Design a project-based learning activity for a specific age group and subject. Define the learning objectives, outline the project tasks, and consider the resources and support needed for students to complete the project successfully. 3. Explore different online tools and platforms that can support flipped classroom instruction. Choose one tool and create a short video tutorial or presentation on how to use it effectively in a flipped learning environment. 4. Analyze a case study of a classroom that successfully implemented differentiated instruction. Identify the strategies and practices that were used to meet the diverse needs of students. Reflect on how you could apply similar approaches in your own classroom. 5. Research emerging technologies in education and identify one that shows promise in enhancing teaching and learning. Write a short proposal arguing for its incorporation in your educational context, considering the potential benefits and addressing potential challenges.

Remember, providing a comprehensive overview of successful educational practices is an ongoing process. By staying informed about the latest research, exchanging ideas with colleagues, and continuously reflecting on your own practice, you can contribute to the growth and improvement of education.

Offering practical strategies for teachers and learners

In this section, we will explore a range of practical strategies that teachers and learners can employ to enhance the learning experience. These strategies are rooted in evidence-based practices and have been proven to be effective in various educational settings. By implementing these strategies, teachers can create engaging and inclusive classrooms, while learners can develop critical thinking skills and deepen their understanding of the subject matter.

Active Learning

Active learning is an approach that emphasizes student participation and engagement in the learning process. It involves learners in activities that promote analysis, synthesis, and evaluation of information, rather than passively receiving information from the teacher. There are several practical strategies that teachers can use to encourage active learning:

- **Classroom discussions:** Teachers can facilitate meaningful discussions by asking open-ended questions, encouraging students to share their opinions, and fostering a respectful environment where all voices are heard. Discussions help students develop communication skills, critical thinking, and the ability to articulate their thoughts effectively.

- **Group work:** Collaborative learning activities, such as group projects or problem-solving tasks, give students the opportunity to work together, share ideas, and learn from one another. Group work promotes teamwork, communication skills, and the ability to negotiate and compromise.

- **Hands-on experiments and simulations:** Engaging learners in practical activities, such as experiments or simulations, allows them to apply theoretical knowledge in a real-world context. These activities promote critical thinking, problem-solving, and active engagement with the subject matter.

- **Role-playing and case studies:** Role-playing exercises and case studies provide learners with the opportunity to analyze and solve complex problems or real-life scenarios. This strategy helps develop analytical skills, decision-making abilities, and empathy towards different perspectives.

By incorporating active learning strategies into their instruction, teachers can create a dynamic and student-centered learning environment that fosters engagement, critical thinking, and collaboration.

Metacognitive Strategies

Metacognition refers to the awareness and understanding of one's own cognitive processes. By developing metacognitive skills, learners become more strategic, reflective, and self-regulated in their approach to learning. Here are some practical strategies that teachers can use to promote metacognition:

- **Explicit instruction on metacognitive strategies:** Teachers can explicitly teach students how to plan, monitor, and evaluate their learning. This includes teaching learners how to set goals, select appropriate strategies, and reflect on their progress. By providing explicit guidance on metacognitive strategies, teachers empower learners to take control of their own learning process.

+ **Think-alouds:** Think-alouds involve the teacher verbalizing their thought process while solving a problem or completing a task. By modeling their thinking process, teachers help students understand how to approach complex problems and make effective decisions. Think-alouds allow learners to see the metacognitive strategies in action and learn how to apply them independently.

+ **Reflection activities:** Reflection activities, such as journaling or group discussions, provide learners with an opportunity to reflect on their learning experiences and identify strengths and areas for improvement. Teachers can encourage learners to reflect on their progress, identify effective learning strategies, and set goals for future learning.

+ **Self-assessment and peer feedback:** By engaging in self-assessment and providing constructive feedback to their peers, learners develop metacognitive skills. Teachers can design rubrics or checklists that help students assess their own work and provide specific feedback on areas of improvement. Peer feedback encourages learners to reflect on their own work and develop a deeper understanding of the subject matter.

By integrating metacognitive strategies into their teaching practices, teachers can empower learners to become active, self-regulated, and lifelong learners.

Differentiation

Differentiation involves tailoring instruction to meet the diverse needs and learning styles of individual learners. By providing differentiated instruction, teachers can ensure that every student has the opportunity to succeed and reach their full potential. Here are some practical strategies for differentiation:

+ **Flexible grouping:** Teachers can group students based on their learning needs and abilities. This allows for targeted instruction and individualized support. Flexible grouping can be done in various ways, such as small group instruction, one-on-one conferences, or peer tutoring.

+ **Varied instructional materials:** Teachers can provide a range of resources and materials to accommodate different learning styles and preferences. This may include visuals, videos, hands-on activities, or audio recordings. Varied instructional materials ensure that learners can access and engage with the content in a way that best suits their learning style.

+ **Alternative assessments:** Teachers can offer multiple options for assessing student learning. This allows students to demonstrate their understanding in ways that align with their strengths and interests. Alternative assessments may include projects, presentations, portfolios, or performance-based assessments.

+ **Scaffolded instruction:** Scaffolding involves providing support and guidance to students as they learn new concepts or skills. Teachers can break down complex tasks into smaller, manageable steps, and gradually remove supports as students gain proficiency. Scaffolding helps students build confidence, develop independence, and achieve success.

By implementing differentiation strategies, teachers can create a learning environment that recognizes and values the diversity of learners, promotes inclusivity, and ensures that each student has an equal opportunity to succeed.

Incorporating these practical strategies into teaching and learning environments can greatly enhance educational outcomes. By promoting active learning, metacognitive strategies, and differentiation, teachers can empower learners to become active, engaged, and self-directed learners. These strategies not only support academic achievement but also foster critical thinking, problem-solving skills, and a lifelong love for learning. By applying these practices, teachers and learners can create positive and transformative educational experiences.

Highlighting the impact of cutting-edge research on education

In recent years, the field of education has been greatly influenced by cutting-edge research, which has led to significant advancements in teaching and learning practices. This section will explore the various ways in which research has positively impacted education, shedding light on the innovative strategies and techniques that have emerged as a result. By highlighting the impact of this research, educators will be inspired to embrace new approaches and implement evidence-based practices in their classrooms.

One of the key areas of research that has influenced education is cognitive science. Cognitive science examines the processes of learning, memory, attention, and problem-solving, providing valuable insights into how students acquire and retain knowledge. Researchers have discovered effective learning strategies, such as spaced repetition and retrieval practice, which have proven to enhance long-term retention. For example, studies have shown that spacing out the practice of new information over time, rather than cramming it all at once, leads to better long-term retention and transfer of knowledge. Furthermore, regular retrieval practice, which involves actively recalling information from memory, strengthens learning and increases the likelihood of retaining information in the long run.

Another area of cutting-edge research that has had a significant impact on education is educational psychology. This interdisciplinary field investigates the psychological processes involved in teaching and learning, providing valuable insights into factors that affect motivation, engagement, and academic achievement. Researchers have identified the importance of creating a supportive and inclusive classroom environment, where students feel valued and motivated to learn. By understanding the significance of factors such as autonomy, self-efficacy, and relatedness, educators can design instructional strategies that foster a positive learning environment and promote student success.

Research in the field of educational technology has also revolutionized teaching and learning. With the rapid advancement of technology, researchers have explored innovative ways to integrate digital tools and resources into the classroom. For instance, the use of educational apps, online simulations, and virtual reality experiences can provide immersive and interactive learning opportunities for students. Moreover, technology has made it possible to personalize instruction, tailoring learning experiences to meet the individual needs and preferences of students. By leveraging cutting-edge technologies, educators can create engaging and dynamic learning environments that enhance student motivation and achievement.

In addition to cognitive science, educational psychology, and educational technology, research from various other disciplines has shaped modern education. For instance, studies from the field of neuroscience have deepened our understanding of brain development and its implications for learning. This knowledge has led to the development of neuroscience-informed instructional strategies, such as multisensory learning and brain-compatible teaching. Similarly, research in the field of assessment and feedback has provided valuable insights into effective evaluation practices, enabling educators to provide meaningful feedback that supports student learning and growth.

It is important for educators to stay abreast of cutting-edge research in education to continually enhance their teaching practices. By attending conferences, engaging in professional development opportunities, and actively seeking out research literature, educators can access the latest findings and evidence-based practices. Furthermore, collaboration and partnerships between researchers and educators can facilitate the translation of research into practical strategies and classroom interventions.

While research has undoubtedly had a positive impact on education, it is important to acknowledge the challenges and limitations associated with its implementation. In some cases, research findings may be conflicting or context-specific, requiring educators to critically evaluate and adapt strategies to suit their unique classroom environments. Additionally, not all educators may have the resources or support necessary to implement research-based practices fully. Therefore, it is crucial to promote a culture of research and provide educators with the necessary training and resources to effectively integrate research findings into their teaching practices.

In conclusion, cutting-edge research has had a transformative impact on education, providing educators with valuable insights and evidence-based strategies to enhance teaching and learning. From cognitive science to educational psychology, and from educational technology to neuroscience, researchers from a range of disciplines have contributed to the advancement of education. By embracing research, educators can stay at the forefront of innovative practices and create dynamic learning environments that meet the needs of their students. Through ongoing collaboration between researchers and educators, we can continue to harness the power of research to drive positive change in education.

Structure of the Book

Overview of chapters and their contents

In this section, we will provide an overview of the chapters included in this book and outline their contents. Each chapter focuses on different aspects of educational success stories, offering practical strategies, transformative techniques, and cutting-edge research to shape modern learning and teaching. Let's dive into each chapter and explore what they have to offer:

Chapter 1: Transformative Techniques

This chapter delves into transformative techniques that have the potential to revolutionize the way we approach teaching and learning. It is divided into three sections, each exploring a different transformative technique and its applications.

Section 1, titled "Personalized Learning," examines personalized learning as an approach to tailor education to individual students' needs. It defines personalized learning, provides principles for implementation, showcases successful initiatives, discusses challenges, and explores future trends.

Section 2 focuses on "Project-Based Learning." This subsection explores the benefits of project-based learning, outlines the steps for designing and implementing project-based learning activities, shares success stories from various educational contexts, and provides best practices and recommendations.

Section 3 explores the "Flipped Classroom Model." It explains the concept of the flipped classroom, offers strategies for preparing and delivering flipped lessons, presents case studies of successful implementation, discusses challenges, and delves into alternative models of flipped learning.

Chapter 2: Practical Strategies for Effective Teaching and Learning

This chapter focuses on practical strategies that can enhance teaching and learning outcomes. It is divided into three sections, each addressing different strategies for effective teaching and learning.

Section 1, titled "Classroom Management," outlines strategies for establishing an inclusive and positive classroom environment. It covers effective behavior management techniques, promoting student engagement and motivation, addressing individual needs and learning differences, and preventing and managing conflicts.

Section 2 delves into "Differentiated Instruction," an approach that tailors instruction to meet the diverse needs of learners. It explores the principles of differentiated instruction, offers strategies for designing and delivering differentiated lessons, presents successful implementation examples, and discusses assessing and adapting instruction for diverse learners.

Section 3, titled "Technology Integration," focuses on the benefits and challenges of integrating technology into education. It provides strategies for effective technology integration, showcases successful initiatives, evaluates the impact of technology on student achievement, and discusses future trends and emerging technologies.

Chapter 3: The Role of Research in Shaping Modern Education

This chapter explores the role of research in shaping modern education. It is divided into three sections, each addressing different aspects of research in education.

Section 1, titled "Evidence-Based Practice in Education," introduces evidence-based practice and its importance in education. It covers evaluating and using research evidence in decision-making, presents case studies of evidence-based practices, discusses challenges, and promotes a culture of evidence-based practice.

Section 2 focuses on "Educational Neuroscience," exploring the applications of neuroscience in teaching and learning. It discusses brain development and its implications for education, neuroscience-informed instructional strategies, ethical considerations, and potential risks, as well as future directions and challenges.

Section 3 addresses "Assessment and Feedback" in education. It highlights the importance of assessment and feedback, presents different assessment types and their uses, offers strategies for providing effective feedback, showcases innovations in assessment and feedback practices, and discusses challenges and ensuring fairness.

Chapter 4: Case Studies in Educational Success

This chapter presents case studies of educational success stories from various educational contexts. It is divided into three sections, each focusing on a different educational level or area.

Section 1, titled "K-12 Education," presents success stories in elementary, middle, and high school education. It highlights innovative practices, strategies for addressing equity and diversity, and future directions and challenges in K-12 education.

Section 2 focuses on "Higher Education," showcasing transformative practices in undergraduate and graduate education. It discusses integrating research and teaching, strategies for enhancing student engagement and retention, and innovations in online and blended learning.

Section 3 explores "Vocational and Adult Education," providing effective strategies for vocational education and training. It also shares success stories and practical strategies for adult learning, discusses bridging the gap between education and workforce demands, promoting lifelong learning and reskilling, and addressing challenges and opportunities.

By exploring these chapters, readers will gain valuable insights into successful educational practices, practical strategies for teaching and learning, the role of research in shaping modern education, and inspiring case studies of educational success.

Key themes and topics covered in each chapter

In this section, we will provide an overview of the key themes and topics covered in each chapter of the book "Educational Success Stories: How Transformative

Techniques, Practical Strategies, and Cutting-Edge Research Shape Modern Learning and Teaching". This will give readers a sense of the breadth and depth of the content presented in the book.

Chapter 1 focuses on transformative techniques in education. It explores three key techniques: personalized learning, project-based learning, and the flipped classroom model. Subsection 1 delves into personalized learning, including its definition, principles, and strategies for implementation. Subsection 2 highlights project-based learning, discussing its benefits and steps for designing and implementing such activities. Subsection 3 explores the flipped classroom model, providing an overview of its principles and strategies for preparing and delivering flipped lessons. This chapter also includes case studies, challenges, potential solutions, and future trends associated with each technique.

Moving on to Chapter 2, the focus shifts to practical strategies for effective teaching and learning. Section 1 explores classroom management, covering topics such as establishing an inclusive and positive classroom environment, effective behavior management strategies, promoting student engagement and motivation, addressing individual needs and learning differences, and preventing and managing conflicts. Section 2 delves into differentiated instruction, discussing its principles, strategies for designing and delivering differentiated lessons, successful implementation in various subjects, assessing and adapting instruction, and ensuring equity. Another key theme covered in Section 3 is technology integration, which includes topics like benefits and challenges, strategies for effective integration, examples of successful initiatives, evaluating impact, and future trends.

Chapter 3 highlights the role of research in shaping modern education. Section 1 focuses on evidence-based practice, covering its introduction, importance in education, evaluating and using research evidence, case studies of evidence-based practices, challenges, and promoting a culture of evidence-based practice. Section 2 introduces educational neuroscience, discussing its applications in teaching and learning, brain development and implications for education, neuroscience-informed instructional strategies, ethical considerations, and future directions. Section 3 delves into assessment and feedback, covering topics such as the importance of assessment and feedback, different types of assessments, strategies for providing effective feedback, innovations in assessment and feedback practices, and addressing challenges and ensuring fairness.

In the final chapter, Chapter 4, readers will find case studies in educational success. Section 1 focuses on K-12 education, highlighting success stories and strategies in elementary education, innovative practices in middle school education, success stories and strategies in high school education, addressing equity and diversity, and future directions and challenges. Section 2 shifts the focus to higher education, discussing transformative practices in undergraduate teaching and learning, success stories in graduate education, integrating research and teaching, enhancing student engagement and retention, innovations in online and blended learning. Section 3 explores vocational and adult education, covering effective strategies for vocational education and training, success stories and practical strategies in adult learning, bridging the gap between education and workforce demands, promoting lifelong learning and re-skilling in the workplace, and challenges and opportunities.

Throughout the book, readers will find a variety of examples, case studies, and practical strategies that can be directly applied in educational contexts. The combination of transformative techniques, practical strategies, and research-based insights provides a well-rounded approach to understanding and improving education. Whether you are a teacher, learner, or education policymaker, this book offers valuable insights and guidance for achieving educational success.

Importance of Educational Success Stories

Motivating teachers and learners

Motivation plays a crucial role in the success of both teachers and learners. When teachers are motivated, they are more likely to be enthusiastic, creative, and dedicated, which in turn positively impacts student achievement. Similarly, when learners are motivated, they are more engaged, curious, and willing to put in the effort to learn and succeed. In this section, we will explore various strategies and techniques to motivate both teachers and learners in the educational setting.

Understanding the importance of motivation

Motivation is a driving force that pushes teachers and learners to take action, persevere through challenges, and strive for excellence. It is important to recognize that motivation is not solely dependent on external factors such as rewards or punishments; it is largely driven by internal factors such as personal interests, goals, values, and the belief in one's ability to succeed. When teachers and learners are motivated, they are more likely to actively participate in the learning process, demonstrate a positive attitude toward learning, and achieve higher levels of success.

Key theories and principles of motivation

Several theories and principles provide insights into the factors that influence motivation in the educational context. One such theory is Self-Determination Theory (SDT), which proposes that individuals are motivated when their basic psychological needs for autonomy, competence, and relatedness are satisfied. According to SDT, providing learners with choices, opportunities for skill development, and a sense of belonging can enhance their motivation to learn.

Another theory is Achievement Goal Theory (AGT), which suggests that learners' motivation is influenced by their goal orientation. Individuals with a mastery goal orientation are motivated by the desire to develop their competence and master new skills, while those with a performance goal orientation are motivated by the desire to demonstrate their ability and outperform others. Teachers can foster a mastery goal orientation by emphasizing the importance of effort, growth, and learning from mistakes.

Furthermore, the Expectancy-Value Theory highlights the role of expectancy beliefs (the belief that effort leads to success) and task values (the importance and interest of a task) in motivating learners. Teachers can enhance learners' motivation by creating a supportive and challenging learning environment that promotes the belief in their ability to succeed and the value of the learning tasks.

Strategies for motivating teachers

1. Professional development opportunities: Offering ongoing professional development opportunities for teachers can enhance their knowledge, skills, and expertise. This can be in the form of workshops, online courses, conferences, and collaboration with colleagues. Providing teachers with the opportunity to learn and grow can reignite their passion for teaching and motivate them to explore new strategies and approaches.

2. Recognition and appreciation: Recognizing and appreciating the hard work and dedication of teachers can go a long way in motivating them. This can be done through formal recognition programs, acknowledging their achievements publicly, or simply expressing gratitude for their contributions. Feeling valued and appreciated can boost teachers' morale and motivate them to continue making a positive impact on their students.

3. Autonomy and empowerment: Providing teachers with the autonomy to make decisions and be creative in their teaching can increase their sense of ownership and motivation. Teachers should have the freedom to choose

instructional materials, design learning activities, and tailor their teaching methods to meet the needs of their students.

4. Collaboration and support: Encouraging collaboration among teachers and providing them with support from colleagues and administrators can foster a sense of community and motivation. Teachers can learn from each other, share best practices, and collectively problem-solve. Additionally, emotional support and mentorship can help reduce feelings of isolation and burnout.

Strategies for motivating learners

1. Establishing relevance: Connecting the content being taught to real-world examples and students' interests can make learning more meaningful and engaging. Teachers can demonstrate the practical applications of the knowledge and skills being taught, allowing learners to see the relevance and value of what they are learning.

2. Providing choice and autonomy: Allowing learners to have a say in their learning can boost their motivation. Teachers can provide options for assignments, projects, or topics to study, enabling learners to pursue their interests and take ownership of their learning. This cultivates a sense of autonomy and responsibility, increasing motivation.

3. Setting challenging yet attainable goals: Setting clear, specific, and challenging goals can motivate learners to strive for excellence. Teachers can work with learners to establish realistic goals that are within their reach and provide appropriate support and feedback to help them progress toward those goals. Celebrating achievements along the way can further enhance motivation.

4. Providing feedback and recognition: Regular and constructive feedback is essential in motivating learners. Teachers should provide timely and specific feedback that focuses on effort, progress, and areas for improvement. Additionally, recognizing and celebrating the achievements of learners, both in academic and non-academic domains, can boost their motivation and self-confidence.

5. Incorporating active and engaging learning experiences: Engaging learners in hands-on, interactive, and collaborative activities can enhance their motivation. This can involve group projects, discussions, simulations, role-plays, and other experiential learning activities. Integrating technology, gamification, and multimedia can also make learning more interactive and appealing to learners.

Addressing challenges in motivation

Motivating teachers and learners is not without its challenges. Some common challenges include:

1. Lack of interest or relevance: If learners do not perceive the content to be interesting or relevant, their motivation may wane. Teachers need to find ways to connect the content to learners' interests and demonstrate its applicability to real-life situations.

2. External pressure and standardized testing: The emphasis on high-stakes testing and external pressure to meet certain standards can undermine intrinsic motivation. It is important to balance the need for accountability with fostering a love for learning and intrinsic motivation.

3. Individual differences: Learners have unique personalities, learning styles, and motivations. Teachers should be aware of these individual differences and strive to provide personalized and differentiated learning experiences to meet diverse needs.

4. Lack of support or resources: Teachers may face challenges in motivating their students due to limited support or resources. It is crucial for educational institutions to provide teachers with the necessary resources, professional development opportunities, and a supportive school culture to foster motivation.

5. Fear of failure: Learners may be afraid of making mistakes or failing, which can hinder their motivation to take risks and challenge themselves. Teachers should create a safe and supportive learning environment that encourages risk-taking, embraces mistakes as learning opportunities, and emphasizes growth mindset.

Conclusion

Motivating teachers and learners is essential for creating a positive and effective learning environment. By understanding the importance of motivation, applying key theories and principles, and implementing strategies such as professional development, recognition, relevance, choice, and feedback, educators can inspire and empower both themselves and their students. Addressing challenges and supporting teachers and learners in their motivation journey is crucial for ensuring educational success and fostering a lifelong love for learning.

Inspiring innovation and creativity in the classroom

Inspiring innovation and creativity in the classroom is a vital aspect of modern education. It encourages students to think critically, solve problems, and explore new ideas. By fostering creativity, teachers can empower students to become active participants in their own learning journey. This section explores the importance of inspiring innovation and creativity in the classroom and provides practical strategies to achieve this goal.

The Importance of Innovation and Creativity

Innovation and creativity are essential skills for the 21st century. The world is rapidly changing, and the ability to adapt, think outside the box, and come up with novel solutions is crucial. By inspiring innovation and creativity in the classroom, we equip students with the necessary skills to thrive in an ever-evolving society.

Moreover, fostering innovation and creativity enhances student engagement and motivation. When students are encouraged to explore and create, they become more invested in their learning. This, in turn, leads to improved academic performance and a deeper understanding of the subject matter.

Strategies for Inspiring Innovation and Creativity

1. Provide open-ended and challenging tasks: Assigning tasks that have multiple solutions or require critical thinking can stimulate innovation and creativity. For example, instead of giving students a specific topic to write about, allow them to choose their own and encourage them to think outside conventional boundaries.

2. Encourage divergent thinking: Divergent thinking is the ability to generate multiple ideas or solutions to a problem. Encourage students to brainstorm and explore different perspectives. This can be done through activities such as brainstorming sessions, mind mapping, or group discussions.

3. Foster a supportive and inclusive classroom environment: Students are more likely to take risks and express their creativity in a safe and supportive environment. Encourage collaboration, celebrate diversity, and provide constructive feedback to create an atmosphere that nurtures innovation and creativity.

4. Incorporate real-world connections: Connect classroom content to real-world applications to inspire students' creativity. Show them how the knowledge and skills they acquire can be applied in practical situations. This can be done through field trips, guest speakers, or project-based learning activities.

5. Integrate technology: Technology can be a powerful tool for fostering innovation and creativity. Encourage students to use digital tools for research,

collaboration, and creating multimedia projects. Platforms like coding apps, graphic design software, and video editing tools can unleash their creative potential.

6. Promote autonomy and self-expression: Provide students with choices and opportunities to express their creativity in different forms. Allow them to take ownership of their learning process and explore their interests and strengths. This can be achieved through project-based learning, individual research projects, or creative assignments.

7. Emphasize the process, not just the outcome: Encourage students to embrace the learning process and value their efforts, even if the outcome is not perfect. By focusing on the process, students become more willing to take risks, learn from failures, and continuously improve their ideas and creations.

Unconventional Idea: The Power of Failure

Failure is often seen as something negative, but it can be a powerful catalyst for innovation and creativity. By reframing failure as a learning opportunity, teachers can inspire students to take risks and think creatively. Encourage students to embrace failure as a stepping stone towards success and to view mistakes as valuable lessons. Highlighting stories of famous failures and their subsequent achievements can serve as a powerful motivational tool.

Example: The Innovation Hour

The Innovation Hour, also known as "Genius Hour" or "Passion Projects," is a popular strategy to inspire innovation and creativity in the classroom. This practice allows students to dedicate a set amount of time each week or month to work on a project of their choice. These projects can be related to any topic that sparks their interest, whether it's writing a novel, creating a website, or conducting scientific experiments. The Innovation Hour promotes self-directed learning, encourages inquiry, and fosters creativity by giving students the freedom to explore their passions and tackle real-world problems.

Resources and Tools

Here are some resources and tools that can assist teachers in inspiring innovation and creativity in the classroom:

- TeachThought: A website offering articles, videos, and resources on innovative teaching strategies and creativity in education. (Website: https://www.teachthought.com/)

- TED-Ed: An educational platform that provides videos and lessons on a wide range of topics, promoting creativity and critical thinking. (Website: `https://ed.ted.com/`)
- Adobe Spark: A suite of creative tools that allows students to create and share visual stories, web pages, and videos. (Website: `https://spark.adobe.com/`)
- Breakout EDU: A platform providing immersive games and activities that foster problem-solving, critical thinking, and collaboration. (Website: `https://www.breakoutedu.com/`)
- Khan Academy: An online learning platform offering a variety of interactive lessons and exercises on various subjects, encouraging personalized learning. (Website: `https://www.khanacademy.org/`)

Exercise: The Innovation Challenge

To inspire innovation and creativity, organize an Innovation Challenge in your classroom. Provide students with a problem or a broad theme and challenge them to come up with innovative solutions or creative projects. Encourage them to think critically, collaborate, and explore unconventional ideas. Allocate dedicated time for brainstorming, planning, and creating prototypes or presentations. Celebrate the process and showcase the innovative projects to the class or school community. Reflect on the experience and discuss the lessons learned from embracing innovation and creativity.

Caveats

While inspiring innovation and creativity has numerous benefits, it is important to consider these caveats:

1. Assessment: Measuring innovation and creativity can be challenging. Design assessment methods that capture the essence of these skills, such as rubrics that evaluate problem-solving, critical thinking, and originality.

2. Time constraints: Inspiring innovation and creativity requires time. Ensure that the curriculum allows for flexibility and provides opportunities for students to explore their ideas and passions.

3. Different learning styles: Recognize that students have different learning styles and preferences. Provide varied approaches and resources to cater to diverse learners and their creative expressions.

4. Cultural considerations: Respect cultural differences and encourage students to integrate their cultural backgrounds into their creative projects. Celebrate diversity and create a multicultural learning environment.

Inspiring innovation and creativity in the classroom is a powerful way to prepare students for the challenges and opportunities of the future. By implementing strategies, fostering a supportive environment, and embracing failure as a learning experience, educators can ignite the creative spark in every student. Through innovative thinking and creative problem-solving, students become agents of positive change, contributing to a more innovative and dynamic society.

Promoting Positive Change in Educational Systems

In order to promote positive change in educational systems, it is important to recognize the challenges and barriers that hinder progress and implement strategies that address these issues effectively. This section will explore some of the key challenges faced by educational systems and provide practical solutions for promoting positive change.

Challenges in Educational Systems

1. Limited Resources: Many educational systems face resource constraints, including inadequate funding, lack of infrastructure, and limited access to technology. These limitations can impede the delivery of quality education and limit opportunities for students.

2. Inequality and Inequity: Educational systems often struggle with addressing inequality and inequity, which can result from disparities in funding, access to educational resources, and social factors. This can lead to unequal outcomes and hinder the overall development of students.

3. Outdated Curriculum and Teaching Methods: The traditional curriculum and teaching methods in many educational systems may not align with the needs of modern learners. Outdated content, rote memorization, and teacher-centered approaches can hinder student engagement and limit learning outcomes.

4. Standardized Testing Pressure: High-stakes standardized testing can create undue pressure on students, teachers, and schools. The focus on test scores may lead to a narrow curriculum and teaching to the test, which may not effectively prepare students for real-world challenges.

Strategies for Promoting Positive Change

1. Equitable Resource Allocation: Ensuring equitable distribution of resources is crucial for promoting positive change in educational systems. This includes allocating adequate funding, improving infrastructure, and providing access to technology and learning resources for all students and schools.

2. Inclusive and Diverse Education: Educational systems should strive to create inclusive and diverse learning environments that cater to the needs of all learners. This involves embracing diverse perspectives, cultures, and learning styles to promote understanding, empathy, and equity in education.

3. Curriculum Innovation: Rethinking and innovating the curriculum is essential for promoting positive change. Educational systems should focus on developing relevant and future-oriented curricula that emphasize critical thinking, problem-solving, creativity, and collaboration. Integrating interdisciplinary content and real-world applications can enhance student engagement and prepare them for the challenges of the modern world.

4. Student-Centered Approaches: Shifting the focus from teacher-centered to student-centered approaches is vital for promoting positive change. Educational systems should prioritize personalized and differentiated instruction, allowing students to take ownership of their learning and explore their interests and talents. This can enhance engagement, motivation, and overall learning outcomes.

5. Authentic Assessment: Moving away from solely relying on standardized testing and embracing authentic assessment methods can promote positive change in educational systems. Authentic assessments, such as project-based assessments, portfolios, and performance tasks, provide a more comprehensive and holistic view of student learning and can foster critical thinking, problem-solving, and creativity.

Examples and Case Studies

1. Finland's Education System: Finland is often regarded as an example of a successful educational system that promotes positive change. Their focus on equity, student-centered approaches, and a holistic curriculum has led to consistently high student outcomes.

2. Project-Based Learning in California Schools: Many schools in California have adopted project-based learning as a way to promote positive change. By engaging students in real-world projects, they provide opportunities for collaboration, critical thinking, and problem-solving.

Resources for Further Exploration

1. "Equity and Excellence in Education: Towards Maximal Learning Opportunities for All Students" by UNESCO: This publication explores the importance of equity in education and offers strategies for promoting positive change.

2. "Learner-Centered Teaching: Five Key Changes to Practice" by Maryellen Weimer: This book provides practical guidance for implementing learner-centered approaches in the classroom.

3. "Deeper Learning: How Eight Innovative Public Schools Are Transforming Education in the Twenty-First Century" by Monica Martinez and Dennis McGrath: This book showcases real-world examples of schools promoting positive change through innovative teaching and learning practices.

Conclusion

Promoting positive change in educational systems is crucial for ensuring optimal learning outcomes and fostering the holistic development of students. By addressing challenges such as limited resources, inequality, outdated teaching methods, and high-stakes testing, and implementing strategies like equitable resource allocation, inclusive and diverse education, curriculum innovation, student-centered approaches, and authentic assessment, educational systems can create an environment that maximizes learning opportunities for all students. Through continuous efforts and a commitment to educational improvement, positive change can be achieved, leading to a brighter future for learners worldwide.

Chapter 1: Transformative Techniques

Section 1: Personalized Learning

Subsection 1: Definition and principles of personalized learning

Personalized learning is an approach to education that tailors instruction and learning experiences to meet the individual needs, interests, and aspirations of each learner. It recognizes that every student is unique and learns at their own pace and in their own way. The principles of personalized learning revolve around creating a student-centered environment that fosters engagement, motivation, and deep understanding of concepts.

The key principles of personalized learning include:

1. Individualized Instruction: Personalized learning emphasizes the customization of instruction based on each learner's strengths, weaknesses, learning style, and interests. This involves providing students with different pathways to achieve their learning goals. For example, if a student has a strong visual learning preference, the teacher may incorporate more visual aids and resources into their lessons.

2. Learner Autonomy: Personalized learning empowers students to take ownership of their learning journey. It encourages them to set goals, manage their time effectively, and make choices that align with their personal interests and aspirations. By providing learners with autonomy, personalized learning promotes intrinsic motivation and a sense of agency in the learning process.

3. Competency-Based Progression: Rather than focusing on seat time or fixed timelines, personalized learning emphasizes mastery of essential skills and knowledge. Students progress at their own pace and advance to the next level of content only when they have demonstrated mastery. This approach ensures that

learners have a solid foundation before moving on to more complex concepts.

4. Flexible Learning Environments: Personalized learning acknowledges that students have different preferences for where and how they learn best. It allows for flexibility in the learning environment, whether that's in a traditional classroom, a virtual setting, or a combination of both. Adaptive technology and online platforms can be used to provide personalized feedback, adapt content to learners' needs, and provide additional practice or enrichment opportunities.

5. Data-Driven Decision Making: Personalized learning utilizes data to inform instructional decisions and track students' progress. Teachers collect and analyze data on individual student performance to identify areas of strength and areas that need improvement. This data-driven approach enables teachers to provide targeted support, offer personalized interventions, and adjust teaching strategies to meet individual needs effectively.

6. Collaboration and Differentiated Instruction: Personalized learning promotes collaboration among students and teachers to enhance learning experiences. It recognizes that learners may require different levels and types of support. Teachers differentiate instruction by providing various resources, materials, and activities to accommodate diverse learners' needs. Collaborative group work, peer learning, and one-on-one coaching are common practices in personalized learning environments.

Overall, personalized learning is not just about using technology or implementing individualized instruction. It is an instructional approach that recognizes and caters to the diverse needs and interests of learners while fostering their autonomy, mastery, and collaboration skills. By prioritizing individuality and personal growth, personalized learning cultivates a love for learning, enhances student outcomes, and prepares learners for success in the modern world.

Example: Applying personalized learning principles in a mathematics classroom

In a mathematics classroom, personalized learning can play a vital role in addressing students' diverse needs and promoting a deep understanding of mathematical concepts. Here's an example of how personalized learning principles can be applied:

A teacher starts by assessing each student's prior knowledge and understanding of foundational mathematical concepts. Based on the assessment results, the teacher creates personalized learning plans for each student, identifying specific areas of focus and setting individualized learning goals.

During instruction, the teacher incorporates various instructional strategies to cater to different learning styles and preferences. For visual learners, the teacher uses diagrams, charts, and manipulatives to illustrate mathematical concepts.

Auditory learners benefit from discussions, explanations, and verbal problem-solving exercises, while kinesthetic learners engage in hands-on activities or real-world applications of mathematical concepts.

To promote learner autonomy, the teacher offers students choices in how they demonstrate their understanding of mathematical concepts. Some students may prefer written explanations, others may create presentations or solve real-world problems. The teacher provides feedback to guide students and help them reflect on their strengths and areas for improvement.

The classroom environment encourages collaboration, with students working in pairs or small groups to solve complex problems. Peer learning and peer assessment are incorporated, where students provide feedback and support to each other. This not only fosters collaboration but also reinforces learning as students share their understanding and thought processes.

Throughout the learning process, the teacher collects data on student progress and uses this information to adjust instruction and provide targeted interventions. Regular formative assessments help identify areas where students may need additional support or where they are ready to move on to more challenging concepts and skills.

By implementing personalized learning principles in mathematics instruction, students have the opportunity to develop a deep understanding of mathematical concepts, build problem-solving skills, and cultivate a growth mindset. They become active participants in their learning, driven by their own interests, abilities, and aspirations.

Resources for personalized learning:

- The Future of Personalized Learning (report) by Digital Promise: This report offers insights into the benefits and challenges of personalized learning and provides examples of successful implementation in schools.

- The Learner-Centered Innovation Guide by Katie Martin: This book offers practical strategies and ideas for implementing personalized learning in the classroom and creating learner-centered environments.

- Khan Academy (website): Khan Academy provides a vast collection of free online resources and lessons that can be personalized to meet each student's needs. It covers various subjects, including mathematics, science, history, and more.

- Edutopia (website): Edutopia offers a wealth of resources and articles on personalized learning, showcasing innovative practices, research, and success stories from educators around the world.

- ASCD (Association for Supervision and Curriculum Development) (website): ASCD provides resources, webinars, and publications related to personalized learning. They offer insights and practical advice for educators looking to implement personalized learning effectively.

- Teach to One: Math (program): Teach to One is a personalized learning program specifically designed for mathematics instruction. It utilizes adaptive technology and data-driven insights to deliver personalized math instruction to students.

- TED Talks: TED Talks feature speakers from various backgrounds discussing topics related to education, including personalized learning. These talks can provide inspiration and insights into the potential of personalized learning in transforming education.

Personalized learning is a powerful approach that can revolutionize education by placing the needs and aspirations of learners at the center. By embracing the principles of personalized learning, educators can create engaging and meaningful learning experiences that support the success and growth of every student.

Subsection 2: Strategies for implementing personalized learning

Personalized learning is an approach to education that tailors the learning experience to meet the unique needs, interests, and abilities of each student. It recognizes that every learner is different and requires individualized support to achieve their full potential. In this subsection, we will explore various strategies for implementing personalized learning in the classroom.

1. Differentiated Instruction: - Differentiated instruction is a key strategy in personalized learning. It involves adjusting the content, process, and products of learning to accommodate the diverse needs of students. Teachers can differentiate instruction by: - Providing choice: Offering students a range of options for demonstrating their understanding of the content. For example, allowing students to choose between writing an essay, creating a presentation, or designing a project. - Adapting materials: Modifying resources to ensure they are accessible to all students. This could involve providing additional support materials for struggling learners or extending challenges for advanced students. - Grouping students: Creating flexible groups based on students' readiness levels, interests, or learning preferences. Students can work collaboratively or independently, depending on their needs. - Individualizing goals: Setting personalized learning goals for each student based on their strengths, areas for improvement, and personal interests.

2. Personal Learning Plans: - Personal learning plans (PLPs) are a valuable tool for implementing personalized learning. PLPs involve collaboratively developing a roadmap for each student's learning journey. Some strategies for creating effective PLPs include: - Goal setting: Encouraging students to set

specific, achievable goals based on their interests and aspirations. These goals can be short-term and long-term, providing a sense of direction for the student. - Regular assessment: Conducting ongoing assessments to monitor student progress and adjust the learning plan accordingly. This could involve formative assessments, self-reflection activities, or peer feedback. - Individual conferences: Meeting with students one-on-one to discuss their progress, challenges, and areas for improvement. These conferences provide an opportunity for personalized feedback and guidance. - Reflection and revision: Encouraging students to reflect on their learning experience, identify what has worked well, and make revisions to their learning plan as needed.

3. Technology Integration: - Technology can play a crucial role in personalized learning by providing adaptive and individualized learning experiences. Some strategies for integrating technology effectively in personalized learning include: - Adaptive learning platforms: Using adaptive software or online platforms that adjust the difficulty level and pace of instruction based on students' performance and progress. These platforms provide personalized feedback and recommendations for further learning. - Online resources and learning tools: Curating a collection of online resources, apps, and interactive tools that cater to a range of learning styles and abilities. Students can access these resources independently, reinforcing personalized learning outside the classroom. - Data-driven instruction: Leveraging data collected through technology tools to inform instructional decisions. Teachers can analyze student performance data, identify trends or areas of improvement, and tailor their instruction accordingly.

4. Student Voice and Choice: - Empowering students to have a voice in their learning journey is a fundamental aspect of personalized learning. Here are some strategies to foster student voice and choice: - Personalized goal setting: Encouraging students to set their own goals and objectives, giving them ownership of their learning. - Student-led conferences: Allowing students to showcase their learning progress to their parents, teachers, and peers. This provides an opportunity for students to articulate their strengths, challenges, and growth areas. - Project-based learning: Engaging students in authentic, real-world projects that allow for creativity, choice, and personalization. Students can choose topics that interest them and develop their own solutions or products. - Student reflection: Providing time and guidance for students to reflect on their learning experiences, strengths, and areas for improvement. Reflection activities can help students understand their learning preferences and set future goals.

It is important to note that implementing personalized learning requires a shift in mindset and pedagogical approaches. Teachers should be flexible, adaptive, and open to experimentation. Collaboration among teachers, administrators, and support staff is essential in creating an environment that supports personalized learning. By leveraging differentiated instruction, personal learning plans, technology integration, and student voice and choice, educators can create an inclusive and engaging learning experience for all students.

Remember, personalized learning is not a one-size-fits-all approach. It is an ongoing process that requires continuous reflection, adjustment, and collaboration to best meet the needs of each individual learner.

Subsection 3: Case studies of successful personalized learning initiatives

In this subsection, we will explore several case studies that demonstrate the success of personalized learning initiatives. These case studies highlight the impact of personalized learning on student engagement, motivation, and academic achievement. Through these success stories, we can gain insights into the practical implementation and outcomes of personalized learning strategies.

Case Study 1: Individualized Learning Plans in Elementary School

One successful personalized learning initiative took place at Meadowbrook Elementary School. The school implemented individualized learning plans (ILPs) for each student, tailoring instruction to meet their unique needs and learning styles. ILPs were created through close collaboration between teachers, parents, and students.

Each ILP included personalized goals, instructional strategies, and assessment methods. Teachers utilized various resources and materials to customize instruction, such as digital programs, hands-on activities, and small group discussions. Students were encouraged to take ownership of their learning by setting goals and reflecting on their progress.

The results were remarkable. Students showed increased engagement, as they were more motivated to learn when their interests and strengths were taken into account. Academic achievement improved, as students were able to work at their own pace and receive targeted support. The implementation of ILPs also fostered a sense of community and collaboration among teachers, parents, and students.

Case Study 2: Adaptive Learning Technology in Middle School

At Oakridge Middle School, personalized learning was enhanced through the use of adaptive learning technology. This technology, incorporated into the classroom setting, provided students with tailored content and adaptive assessments based on their individual abilities and learning progress.

Teachers used the adaptive learning platform to assign and track personalized learning activities. The platform utilized algorithms to analyze student data and generate adaptive recommendations. Students received immediate feedback and support, enabling them to identify areas of difficulty and access resources for further practice.

The implementation of adaptive learning technology had a significant impact on student achievement. Students showed substantial growth in subject areas where they had previously struggled. The adaptive nature of the technology allowed students to progress at their own pace, promoting a deeper understanding of concepts. Moreover, teachers were able to monitor student progress in real-time and provide targeted interventions when necessary.

Case Study 3: Competency-Based Learning in High School

At Jefferson High School, competency-based learning was implemented to personalize the educational experience for students. Competency-based learning focuses on mastery of specific skills and knowledge, rather than relying solely on traditional grading systems. Students progress through the curriculum by demonstrating proficiency in key competencies.

The implementation began with the identification of essential competencies in each subject area. Students were assessed using a variety of methods, such as projects, presentations, and portfolios. Once a competency was mastered, students could move on to the next, rather than being confined to a fixed timeline.

The results of competency-based learning were impressive. Students exhibited a deeper understanding of the material and a greater ability to apply their knowledge to real-world situations. The flexibility of the approach allowed students to pursue their interests and develop skills at their own pace. Additionally, the focus on mastery rather than grades motivated students to take ownership of their learning and strive for excellence.

Conclusion

These case studies demonstrate the effectiveness of personalized learning in improving student outcomes. By tailoring instruction to meet students' individual needs, personalized learning engages and motivates learners, leading to increased academic achievement. The implementation of personalized learning initiatives can be facilitated through collaborative efforts between teachers, students, and parents, as well as the utilization of adaptive technology and competency-based approaches.

As educators continue to explore innovative practices in personalized learning, it is vital to consider the unique characteristics and needs of each learner. By incorporating personalized learning strategies into educational systems, we can foster a more inclusive, engaging, and successful learning environment for all students.

Subsection 4: Challenges and Potential Solutions in Personalized Learning

Personalized learning offers a promising approach to education by tailoring instruction to meet the unique needs, interests, and learning styles of each individual student. However, like any educational strategy, it comes with its own set of challenges. In this subsection, we will explore the key challenges faced in personalized learning and present potential solutions to address them.

Challenge 1: Implementing Effective Assessment

One of the primary challenges in personalized learning is designing and implementing effective assessments that accurately measure students' progress and growth. Traditional standardized tests may not capture the full range of skills and competencies that personalized learning aims to develop.

Solution: To address this challenge, educators can employ a variety of assessment strategies, including performance-based tasks, portfolios, and self-assessments. These approaches provide a more comprehensive and authentic picture of students' abilities and allow for the evaluation of both content knowledge and transferable skills, such as critical thinking and creativity.

Challenge 2: Managing Time and Resources

Another significant challenge in personalized learning is effectively managing time and resources, especially in large classrooms. With students working on individualized learning paths, teachers must ensure that all students receive the support and guidance they need, often within limited time and resources.

Solution: To address this challenge, teachers can utilize technology tools and platforms that facilitate personalized instruction. Adaptive learning systems, for example, can automatically adjust the difficulty of tasks based on individual student performance, allowing teachers to focus their attention on areas where students require additional support. Additionally, collaborative learning strategies and peer tutoring can help leverage the expertise of students and distribute teacher resources more effectively.

Challenge 3: Addressing Equity and Accessibility

Personalized learning has the potential to exacerbate existing inequities in education if not implemented carefully. There may be disparities in access to technology, resources, and teacher support, leading to unequal learning opportunities.

Solution: To address this challenge, it is crucial to ensure equitable access to technology and resources for all students. Schools can provide devices and internet access to students who do not have them at home, offer extended learning opportunities beyond the school day, and provide additional support for students who need it the most. Additionally, strategies such as differentiated instruction and Universal Design for Learning (UDL) can help accommodate diverse learners and ensure equal access to high-quality education.

Challenge 4: Nurturing Student Autonomy and Ownership

In personalized learning, students are expected to take more responsibility for their learning, make decisions about their learning paths, and set goals. However, fostering student autonomy and ownership can be challenging, especially for students who are accustomed to traditional teacher-centered classrooms.

Solution: To address this challenge, educators can gradually introduce self-directed learning opportunities and provide scaffolding to support students' development of autonomy. Teachers can guide students in goal-setting, reflection, and self-assessment processes, and gradually release control over learning decisions to students. Additionally, promoting a growth mindset and fostering a classroom culture that values student voice and choice can further enhance student ownership in personalized learning environments.

Challenge 5: Professional Development for Teachers

Implementing personalized learning requires a shift in teaching practices, pedagogical approaches, and the role of the teacher. However, many educators may lack the necessary training and support to effectively implement personalized learning strategies.

Solution: To address this challenge, schools and districts should invest in tailored professional development programs that equip teachers with the necessary knowledge, skills, and strategies for personalized learning. This may include training on how to use technology tools effectively, designing personalized learning experiences, and fostering student agency. Collaborative professional learning communities can also serve as a forum for teachers to share best practices, reflect on their experiences, and support each other in implementing personalized learning effectively.

In overcoming these challenges and implementing personalized learning successfully, educators can unlock the potential of each student, support their diverse learning needs, and create an engaging and inclusive learning environment. By embracing innovative approaches and continuously refining their practices, teachers can empower students to become lifelong learners and thrive in the modern world.

Subsection 5: Future trends in personalized learning

Personalized learning has become an integral part of modern education, enabling students to have customized learning experiences that cater to their individual needs, interests, and abilities. As educational technology continues to advance, there are several exciting future trends that have the potential to revolutionize personalized learning even further. In this subsection, we will explore these trends and their implications for the future of education.

Integration of Artificial Intelligence (AI)

Artificial Intelligence (AI) has made significant advancements in recent years and has the potential to transform personalized learning. With AI, educational platforms and systems can collect and analyze vast amounts of student data to provide personalized recommendations, adapt instruction in real-time, and identify areas where students may need additional support.

For example, AI can use data from previous student interactions to design personalized learning paths that are tailored to each individual's learning style and pace. This could involve creating custom-made lesson plans, offering individualized practice exercises, and providing targeted feedback and support.

Furthermore, AI can assist in assessing and tracking student progress, identifying knowledge gaps, and predicting future learning needs. By leveraging machine learning algorithms, AI can continuously refine its recommendations and adapt its strategies based on student performance and feedback, making learning experiences more efficient and effective.

While the integration of AI in personalized learning holds immense potential, it is important to address privacy concerns and ensure that student data is securely collected and used ethically. Additionally, educators should be trained to understand and utilize AI tools effectively to create meaningful learning experiences.

Immersive Virtual Reality (VR) and Augmented Reality (AR)

Another exciting future trend in personalized learning is the integration of immersive technologies like Virtual Reality (VR) and Augmented Reality (AR). These technologies offer unique and engaging learning experiences that can be personalized to meet individual student needs.

VR and AR can transport students to virtual environments, allowing them to explore historical sites, interact with 3D models, and engage in simulations. This immersive experience enhances student engagement and provides opportunities for hands-on learning that may not be possible in traditional classrooms.

For example, in a history class, students can virtually visit ancient civilizations and experience life during different historical eras. In a science class, students can perform virtual experiments and observe complex scientific concepts in action. These experiences allow students to apply their knowledge in real-world contexts, fostering deeper understanding and knowledge retention.

As VR and AR technologies become more affordable and accessible, their integration in personalized learning is expected to increase. However, challenges such as limited content availability and the need for specialized equipment may need to be addressed for widespread adoption.

Adaptive Learning Systems

Adaptive learning systems are an emerging trend in personalized learning that leverage technology to provide individualized instruction based on continuous assessment and learner feedback.

These systems use algorithms to analyze student performance data and adapt instruction in real-time. They can identify areas where students are struggling or excelling and provide targeted interventions or advanced challenges accordingly. By continuously adjusting the difficulty and pace of instruction, adaptive learning systems ensure that students are consistently challenged at their optimal learning level.

Adaptive learning systems can also provide immediate feedback to students, guiding them through the learning process and offering personalized recommendations for improvement. This helps students take ownership of their learning and develop critical thinking and problem-solving skills.

Moreover, adaptive learning systems can support differentiated instruction for diverse groups of students, catering to their varying learning styles, preferences, and strengths. This ensures that every student receives instruction that is tailored to their specific needs and can progress at their own pace.

The integration of adaptive learning systems in personalized learning has the potential to transform education by making learning experiences more engaging, efficient, and effective. However, it is crucial to ensure that these systems are designed ethically and consider the whole learner, not just the academic domain. Educators should also be trained to interpret and utilize the data provided by these systems effectively.

Collaborative Learning and Peer Interaction

Collaborative learning and peer interaction have always been valuable components of the learning process. In the future, personalized learning will continue to emphasize the importance of social interactions and collaboration among students.

While technology is often seen as a solitary endeavor, it can also facilitate collaboration within personalized learning environments. Online platforms and tools enable students to connect with peers, engage in virtual discussions, and collaborate on projects, regardless of their physical location.

Collaborative learning in personalized settings can foster the development of important skills such as communication, teamwork, and problem-solving. Students can benefit from diverse perspectives, learn from each other's experiences, and gain a deeper understanding of content through active engagement with their peers.

Moreover, personalized learning can provide opportunities for peer mentoring and tutoring, where students with advanced knowledge and skills can support their peers who may be struggling. This creates a supportive and inclusive learning environment where students take an active role in helping each other succeed.

It is important for educators to facilitate and foster meaningful collaboration within personalized learning environments. They can design collaborative activities, provide guidance on effective online communication, and establish norms and expectations for respectful and productive interactions.

Addressing Equity and Access

As personalized learning continues to evolve, it is crucial to address equity and access to ensure that all students have equal opportunities to benefit from these innovative approaches.

One future trend in personalized learning is the development of strategies and technologies that support learners from diverse backgrounds and varying levels of access to resources. This includes designing localized curriculum content, providing multilingual support, and integrating assistive technologies for students with disabilities.

Additionally, efforts should be made to bridge the digital divide, ensuring that all students have access to the necessary technology and internet connectivity. This may involve partnerships between schools, communities, and policymakers to provide devices, internet access, and technical support to students who would otherwise be at a disadvantage.

Educators and policymakers should also be mindful of potential biases in personalized learning algorithms and systems. It is important to critically examine and mitigate any unintended consequences, such as reinforcing existing inequities or limiting opportunities for certain groups of students. Regular evaluation and monitoring of personalized learning initiatives can help identify areas for improvement and ensure equitable outcomes.

In conclusion, personalized learning is constantly evolving, and future trends hold great promise for transforming education. The integration of AI, immersive technologies, adaptive learning systems, collaborative learning, and a focus on equity and access have the potential to create engaging and meaningful learning experiences for all students. Educators, researchers, policymakers, and technology developers must work together to harness the full potential of these trends and ensure that personalized learning truly benefits every learner.

Section 2: Project-Based Learning

Subsection 1: Introduction to project-based learning and its benefits

Project-based learning (PBL) is an educational approach that embraces active and engaging learning experiences. It centers around students working on authentic, real-world projects that provide them with opportunities to apply their knowledge and skills in a meaningful context. In this subsection, we will explore the fundamental principles of project-based learning, discuss its benefits, and examine how it can enhance the teaching and learning process.

Principles of Project-Based Learning

At the core of project-based learning are several principles that guide its implementation. These principles serve as a framework for designing and delivering high-quality PBL experiences. Let's explore these principles in detail:

1. **Authenticity:** Projects in PBL should be designed in a way that mirrors real-world problems or challenges. This authenticity helps students make meaningful connections between what they are learning in the classroom and its applications in the real world.

2. **Inquiry-based Learning:** PBL encourages students to be curious, ask questions, and actively seek knowledge to solve problems. It promotes inquiry-based learning, nurturing students' natural curiosity and fostering their ability to independently explore and investigate.

3. **Collaboration:** PBL emphasizes collaborative learning, where students work together in teams to complete projects. This collaborative approach enhances communication, teamwork, and problem-solving skills.

4. **Multidisciplinary Approach:** PBL integrates knowledge and skills from different disciplines, enabling students to see the connections between subjects and develop a holistic understanding. It encourages interdisciplinary thinking and problem-solving.

5. **Sustained Investigation:** Projects in PBL require students to engage in a sustained investigation of a problem or question over an extended period. This encourages deep learning, critical thinking, and problem-solving skills.

Benefits of Project-Based Learning

Project-based learning offers a wide range of benefits for both students and teachers. Let's explore some of the key advantages of implementing PBL in the classroom:

1. **Developing critical thinking skills:** PBL encourages students to analyze, evaluate, and solve complex problems. It promotes critical thinking skills, such as problem identification, analysis, synthesis of information, and evaluation of potential solutions.

2. **Enhancing creativity and innovation:** PBL provides students with opportunities to think creatively, generate new ideas, and approach problems from different perspectives. By engaging in open-ended projects, students can unleash their creativity and develop innovative solutions.

3. **Promoting collaboration and communication:** PBL fosters collaboration and teamwork among students. Working in teams, students learn to communicate

effectively, share ideas, and resolve conflicts. These skills are essential in the modern workplace.

4. **Building a deeper understanding of content:** Through PBL, students delve deeper into the subject matter as they apply their knowledge to solve real-world problems. This approach helps students develop a deeper understanding of concepts and their practical applications.

5. **Increasing motivation and engagement:** PBL offers students a sense of purpose and authenticity in their learning. By working on meaningful projects, students feel more motivated and engaged, leading to increased participation and a positive learning experience.

6. **Developing 21st-century skills:** PBL prepares students for the challenges of the 21st century by developing essential skills such as critical thinking, problem-solving, collaboration, communication, and creativity. These skills are highly valued in today's workforce.

Implementing Project-Based Learning

To successfully implement project-based learning, teachers need to consider various factors. Here are some key considerations for implementing PBL effectively:

1. **Designing authentic and challenging projects:** Projects should be relevant to students' lives and communities, challenging them to apply their knowledge and skills. Authentic projects promote student engagement and motivation.

2. **Establishing clear learning objectives:** Learning objectives should be well-defined and aligned with the curriculum. They should outline the knowledge and skills students will develop through the project.

3. **Providing guidance and support:** Teachers should provide guidance and support to students throughout the project. This can include scaffolding, check-ins, and ongoing feedback to ensure students stay on track and meet their learning goals.

4. **Assessing both process and product:** Assessments should focus on both the process and the final product. Teachers can assess students' critical thinking, problem-solving skills, collaboration, communication, as well as the quality of their final project.

5. **Reflecting on learning experiences:** Reflection is a crucial component of PBL. Students should be given opportunities to reflect on their learning experiences, identify strengths and areas for improvement, and develop a deeper understanding of the content and skills they have acquired.

Example: Project-Based Learning in Science Education

In a science classroom, project-based learning can be used to enhance students' understanding of scientific concepts while fostering their investigative and problem-solving skills.

One example of a project-based learning activity in science could be as follows:

Students are tasked with investigating and designing a sustainable, energy-efficient solution for their school. They would be required to research renewable energy sources, analyze the energy consumption of the school, and propose a project plan that includes the design, implementation, and monitoring of their solution. Throughout the project, students would collect data, conduct experiments, collaborate in teams, and present their findings to their classmates and teachers.

By engaging in this project, students would develop a deeper understanding of renewable energy, energy conservation, data analysis, and collaboration. They would also enhance their critical thinking skills as they evaluate the feasibility and effectiveness of their proposed solution. This project would provide a real-world context for learning scientific concepts and equip students with valuable skills for their future endeavors.

Conclusion

Project-based learning offers a promising approach to education that encourages active, authentic, and collaborative learning experiences. By incorporating the principles of authenticity, inquiry-based learning, collaboration, and sustained investigation, PBL enables students to develop critical thinking skills, enhance creativity, promote collaboration, and deepen their understanding of content. Implementing PBL requires thoughtful planning, clear objectives, guidance, and assessment strategies that evaluate both the process and the final product. Through the meaningful and engaging projects offered by PBL, students can develop the knowledge, skills, and mindset necessary to thrive in the 21st century.

Subsection 2: Steps for designing and implementing project-based learning activities

Project-based learning (PBL) is an instructional approach that engages students in real-world, authentic projects, enabling them to actively explore complex problems and challenges. By designing and implementing effective PBL activities, educators can foster students' critical thinking, problem-solving, collaboration, and communication skills. This subsection will outline the step-by-step process for designing and implementing project-based learning activities.

Step 1: Identify learning goals and standards

Before designing a project-based learning activity, it is essential to clarify the learning goals and align them with relevant academic standards. This step ensures that the projects are not only engaging but also explicitly tied to specific learning outcomes. Consider the desired knowledge, skills, and competencies that students should develop through the project.

For example, in a science class, the learning goal might be for students to understand the scientific method and apply it to investigate a real-world problem. In this case, the project can involve designing and conducting experiments to solve a local environmental issue.

Step 2: Select a real-world problem or challenge

The heart of project-based learning lies in providing students with authentic, real-world problems or challenges to solve. These problems should be relevant to their lives and have meaning beyond the classroom walls. Select a problem or challenge that sparks students' curiosity and motivates them to delve deeply into the project.

For instance, in a history class, the project could involve students researching and presenting alternative perspectives on a historical event or analyzing primary sources to uncover the untold stories of marginalized communities.

Step 3: Define the project scope and timeline

Once the problem or challenge is identified, it is important to define the scope of the project and determine the timeline for completion. This step involves breaking down the project into smaller tasks and setting clear milestones to guide student progress.

Consider the duration of the project, the availability of resources, and any limitations that may impact its implementation. It is crucial to strike a balance between providing sufficient time for students to explore and delve into the project while ensuring that it remains manageable within the given constraints.

Step 4: Scaffold the project with guiding questions

To support students' inquiry and exploration, scaffold the project with guiding questions that will help them investigate and make connections. These questions should prompt critical thinking, problem-solving, and analysis while guiding students towards the project's objectives.

For example, in an English language arts class, the project's guiding questions could focus on exploring the theme of social justice in a novel, such as "How does the author use symbolism to convey ideas about injustice?" or "What are the ethical implications of the protagonist's choices?"

Step 5: Plan and allocate resources

An effective project-based learning activity requires careful planning and allocation of resources. Determine the materials, technology tools, and other resources that students will need to complete the project successfully.

Consider both physical resources, such as books, equipment, and software, as well as human resources, such as experts, mentors, or community partners who can support students in their project work. Ensure that these resources are accessible and available within the given timeframe.

Step 6: Design formative and summative assessments

Assessment is an integral part of project-based learning, enabling educators to evaluate students' progress and provide feedback on their learning. Design both formative and summative assessments that align with the project's learning goals and standards.

Formative assessments, such as checkpoints, reflection journals, and peer feedback, can be implemented throughout the project to monitor students' understanding and guide their ongoing learning. Summative assessments can take the form of a final presentation, report, or portfolio showcasing students' knowledge and skills developed through the project.

Step 7: Facilitate student collaboration and reflection

Project-based learning provides ample opportunities for collaborative work among students. It is crucial to establish a supportive learning environment that encourages collaboration, communication, and teamwork. Design group roles and norms to ensure equal participation and shared responsibilities.

Regularly provide opportunities for students to reflect on their learning, progress, and challenges encountered during the project. Reflection can take various forms, including group discussions, individual journaling, or digital platforms. This reflection process helps students consolidate their learning and make connections between their project experiences and the theoretical content.

Step 8: Assess and provide feedback on the project

As students progress through the project, continuously assess their work and provide timely feedback. This feedback can be given by the teacher, peers, or external experts, depending on the resources available.

Feedback should be constructive, specific, and targeted towards the project's learning goals, highlighting both strengths and areas for improvement. Encourage students to use this feedback to refine their work and deepen their understanding.

Step 9: Celebrate and showcase the project

At the completion of the project, celebrate students' achievements and provide opportunities for them to showcase their work to a wider audience. This can be done through presentations, exhibitions, or community events.

By showcasing their work, students have the chance to reflect on their learning journey, receive recognition for their accomplishments, and inspire others with their creative solutions to real-world problems.

Step 10: Reflect and refine for future projects

Finally, as educators, reflect on the project's effectiveness and its impact on student learning.   Consider the successes and challenges encountered during the implementation and gather feedback from students to inform future iterations of the project.

Continuous improvement is essential, and each project-based learning experience can help educators refine their practice and create even more engaging and impactful learning opportunities for students.

Overall, designing and implementing project-based learning activities requires thoughtful planning, pedagogical expertise, and a focus on real-world relevance. By following these steps, educators can create transformative learning experiences that equip students with the skills and knowledge they need to thrive in the modern world.

Subsection 3: Success stories of project-based learning in different educational contexts

Project-based learning (PBL) has gained significant attention in education for its ability to engage students in active learning experiences and develop their critical thinking, problem-solving, and collaboration skills. In this subsection, we will explore several success stories of PBL in different educational contexts, highlighting the positive outcomes and lessons learned from these projects.

Success Story 1: Solar Energy Project - High School Level

In a high school physics class, students were tasked with designing and building a solar-powered device that could provide a sustainable solution to a real-world problem in their community. Working in teams, they researched the environmental impact of traditional energy sources and explored the potential benefits of solar energy.

The students applied their knowledge of physics and engineering principles to design and construct solar-powered devices such as solar water heaters, solar-powered phone chargers, and solar cookers. They also conducted experiments to test the efficiency and effectiveness of their devices.

Through this project, students not only developed a deep understanding of solar energy concepts but also gained practical skills in project management, data collection, analysis, and presentation. The project culminated in a public exhibition where students showcased their devices and explained their design choices and the scientific principles behind them.

The success of this project was evident in the enthusiasm and engagement of the students. They expressed a sense of ownership and pride in their work, as well as an understanding of the relevance of their learning to real-world issues. The project also fostered collaboration and teamwork among the students, as they worked together to overcome challenges and achieve their goals.

Success Story 2: Virtual Museum - Middle School Level

In a middle school social studies class, students embarked on a project to create a virtual museum showcasing the history and culture of their local community. The project aimed to provide an authentic and immersive learning experience that allowed students to engage with historical artifacts and stories.

Working in small groups, students conducted research, interviewed local residents, and visited relevant historical sites and museums. They used their findings to curate exhibits in the virtual museum, including text, images, videos, and interactive elements.

The project allowed students to explore various aspects of digital media and technology, including graphic design, video editing, and website development. They also developed critical thinking and communication skills as they analyzed and synthesized historical information and effectively conveyed it to a broader audience.

The virtual museum was made accessible to the local community and received positive feedback from residents, who appreciated the effort put into preserving and sharing their shared history. The project not only deepened students' understanding of the importance of local history but also instilled a sense of civic responsibility and community engagement.

Success Story 3: Sustainable Agriculture Project - Elementary School Level

In an elementary school science class, students participated in a project focused on sustainable agriculture. The objective was to teach students about the life cycle of plants, the importance of organic farming, and the impact of agriculture on the environment.

The students were divided into small groups and given a small plot of land on the school grounds to cultivate. They learned about different types of plants, soil composition, and organic farming practices. They planned and planted their own vegetable gardens, taking care of the plants throughout their growth cycle.

As the plants grew, students monitored their progress, collected data, and documented their observations. They also learned about the importance of composting and implemented composting practices in their gardens. At the end of the project, students harvested their crops and shared the produce with their classmates and teachers.

This project not only provided students with hands-on learning experiences but also fostered an appreciation for sustainable agriculture and the benefits of consuming locally grown, organic produce. Students developed skills in observation, data collection, and teamwork.

The project also had a positive impact on the school community, as it initiated conversations about sustainable practices and healthy eating habits. Students became ambassadors for sustainable agriculture, sharing their knowledge and experiences with their families and advocating for environmentally-friendly practices in their communities.

These success stories illustrate the potential of project-based learning to engage students in meaningful educational experiences. Through these projects, students developed not only subject-specific knowledge and skills but also important 21st-century skills such as critical thinking, collaboration, and communication. By connecting their learning to real-world issues and challenges, students developed a deeper understanding of the relevance and applicability of their education.

Implementing project-based learning requires careful planning, clear learning objectives, and appropriate scaffolding for students. Teachers should provide guidance and support throughout the project and facilitate opportunities for reflection and self-assessment. Additionally, projects should be designed to offer opportunities for student choice, creativity, and diverse perspectives.

Project-based learning is an innovative and effective approach to education that prepares students for the complexities of the modern world. By sharing these success stories and providing practical strategies, we hope to inspire educators to incorporate project-based learning into their classrooms and empower students to become active learners and problem solvers.

Subsection 4: Evaluating the Effectiveness of Project-Based Learning

Project-based learning (PBL) has gained significant attention in the field of education for its potential to enhance student engagement, critical thinking, and problem-solving skills. However, it is essential to evaluate the effectiveness of PBL to ensure its impact on student learning outcomes. This subsection focuses on various approaches and strategies for evaluating the effectiveness of PBL in educational settings.

Assessing Student Learning Outcomes

One of the primary goals of evaluating PBL is to determine its impact on student learning outcomes. This assessment involves looking at both the content knowledge gained by students and the development of essential skills during the project. Here are some key strategies for assessing student learning outcomes in PBL:

1. **Rubrics:** Creating clear and specific rubrics is essential to evaluate student performance in PBL. Rubrics can be used to assess both content-based learning objectives and the acquisition of skills such as critical thinking, collaboration, and problem-solving.

2. **Presentations or Exhibitions:** Allowing students to present their projects or showcase their work to an authentic audience provides an opportunity to assess their understanding and ability to effectively communicate their findings.

3. **Sustained Inquiry:** Assessing students' ability to engage in sustained inquiry throughout the project is crucial. This can be evaluated through periodic check-ins, reflections, or the inclusion of inquiry-based tasks or assessments.

4. **Authentic Assessments:** Using authentic assessments, such as performance tasks or real-world scenarios, allows for a more accurate evaluation of students' ability to apply their knowledge and skills gained through PBL.

Measuring Collaboration and Communication Skills

Collaboration and communication skills are vital aspects of PBL that need to be evaluated separately from content knowledge. Here are some approaches to assess these skills:

1. **Peer and Self-Assessment:** Incorporating opportunities for students to assess their own and their peers' collaboration and communication skills can provide valuable insights into their development. This can be done through structured questionnaires, reflection activities, or group evaluations.

2. **Observation and Reflection:** Observing student interactions during group work and providing feedback based on observations can help assess their collaboration and communication skills. Student reflections on their teamwork experiences can also provide valuable insights into their growth over time.

3. **Product Analysis:** Analyzing the quality of student-produced artifacts, such as group reports or presentations, can provide indications of effective collaboration and communication.

Collecting Feedback and Reflecting on the Process

In addition to assessing student learning outcomes and skills, it is essential to collect feedback on the PBL process itself. This feedback can help identify areas of improvement and further refine the implementation of PBL. Here are some strategies for collecting feedback:

1. **Student Surveys:** Administering surveys to collect students' feedback on their experience with PBL can provide valuable insights into their perceptions, engagement levels, and areas of improvement.

2. **Teacher Reflections:** Teachers should engage in reflective practices to evaluate the strengths and weaknesses of PBL implementation. Reflective journaling or group discussions with colleagues can help identify areas for improvement.

3. **Stakeholder Engagement:** Involving parents, administrators, and other stakeholders in the evaluation process can provide diverse perspectives on the effectiveness of PBL.

Addressing Challenges and Ensuring Rigor

Evaluating the effectiveness of PBL presents some unique challenges. Here are ways to address these challenges and ensure the rigor of the evaluation:

1. **Longitudinal Studies:** Conducting longitudinal studies that track students' progress over an extended period can provide a more comprehensive understanding of the impact of PBL on their learning outcomes.

2. **Comparison Groups:** Establishing comparison groups, such as classrooms using traditional teaching methods, can help determine the relative effectiveness of PBL in achieving desired learning outcomes.

3. **Multiple Measures:** Using multiple measures, including both quantitative and qualitative data, ensures a more robust evaluation of the effectiveness of PBL. This could include pre- and post-tests, interviews, student artifacts, and classroom observations.

4. **External Validation:** Seeking external validation through collaboration with researchers or experts in the field can enhance the credibility and rigor of the evaluation process.

Example: Evaluating the Effectiveness of a PBL Initiative

To illustrate the evaluation of PBL, let's consider a hypothetical example of a PBL initiative focused on sustainable energy sources in a high school science class. The evaluation process might involve the following steps:

1. **Developing Rubrics:** Create rubrics that assess both content knowledge (e.g., understanding of renewable energy concepts) and skills (e.g., critical thinking and collaboration).

2. **Assessing Knowledge and Skills:** Administer pre- and post-tests to measure students' content knowledge growth. Incorporate observations, group reflections, and self-assessment to evaluate their collaboration and communication skills.

3. **Analyzing Artifacts:** Evaluate the quality of student-generated artifacts, such as research papers, multimedia presentations, or models, to gauge the depth of understanding and effective communication.

4. **Student Surveys:** Collect feedback from students through surveys to gauge their engagement, perceptions of the project's authenticity, and the impact on their learning experience.

5. **Teacher Reflections:** Engage teachers in reflective practices through journaling or group discussions to identify areas of improvement in the PBL implementation.

By combining these evaluation strategies, educators can gain valuable insights into the effectiveness of PBL in achieving desired learning outcomes and skill development.

Conclusion

Evaluating the effectiveness of project-based learning is crucial to understand its impact on student learning outcomes and skill development. By employing a variety of assessment strategies, including rubrics, authentic assessments, and feedback collection, educators can gauge the effectiveness of PBL and make informed decisions for improvement. Adapting these evaluation approaches to the specific context of PBL initiatives can lead to continuous growth and enhancement of teaching and learning practices.

Remember, effective evaluation is an iterative process that allows for refinements based on feedback and continuous improvement.

Subsection 5: Best practices and recommendations for project-based learning

Project-based learning (PBL) is an effective instructional approach that engages students in real-world problem-solving activities. In this section, we will explore some best practices and recommendations for implementing PBL in the classroom.

1. Start with a driving question: A driving question is a thought-provoking and open-ended question that stimulates students' curiosity and encourages them to explore the topic in-depth. It should be challenging enough to guide the project but not overly complex. For example, in a science class, a driving question could be, "How can we design an environmentally friendly packaging solution?" This question will guide students throughout the project and lead to further investigations.

2. Provide clear guidelines and expectations: It is important to set clear guidelines and expectations for the project. This includes defining the criteria for success, outlining the steps and deadlines, and explaining the assessment criteria. Clear guidelines help students stay focused and understand their roles and responsibilities within the project.

3. Foster collaboration and teamwork: PBL encourages collaboration and teamwork among students. Assigning roles and responsibilities within the project helps distribute the workload and ensures that each team member contributes to the project's success. Encourage open communication, active listening, and compromise among team members. This not only enhances the learning experience but also prepares students for future collaborative work environments.

4. Provide scaffolding and support: PBL can be challenging for some students, especially those who are new to this approach. Providing scaffolding and support throughout the project helps students build their skills and confidence. Offer guidance, resources, and mentorship to assist students in their research, problem-solving, and presentation skills.

5. Emphasize reflection and metacognition: Reflection is a vital component of PBL. Encourage students to reflect on their learning experiences, challenges faced, successes achieved, and lessons learned. Incorporate regular reflection activities such as journals, group discussions, or presentations. These activities promote metacognition, enabling students to think critically about their own thinking and learning processes.

6. Foster authentic assessments: Traditional assessments such as tests and quizzes may not be appropriate for PBL. Instead, focus on authentic assessments that require students to apply their knowledge and skills to real-world situations. These assessments can include presentations, exhibitions, portfolios, or self-evaluations. Authentic assessments provide a more comprehensive measure of students' understanding and abilities.

7. Encourage students' autonomy and ownership: PBL promotes student autonomy and ownership of their learning. Allow students to have choices in selecting project topics, research methods, and presentation formats. This empowers students and increases their motivation and engagement. However, ensure that their choices align with the learning outcomes and objectives of the project.

8. Build connections to real-world contexts: PBL is most effective when students can see the relevance and significance of their work in real-world contexts. Connect the project to real-world issues, challenges, or current events. Invite guest speakers or experts from relevant fields to share their experiences and insights. This helps students understand the practical applications of their learning and fosters a sense of purpose.

9. Encourage reflection on the process: In addition to reflecting on the content and outcomes of the project, encourage students to reflect on the process itself. Ask them to consider what worked well, what challenges they faced, and what improvements they would make for future projects. This reflection on the process helps students develop valuable problem-solving and critical-thinking skills.

10. Continuous improvement and refinement: PBL is a dynamic process that can be refined and improved over time. Encourage ongoing reflection and feedback from students, teachers, and stakeholders to identify areas for improvement. This feedback loop ensures that future projects can be even more engaging and effective at promoting deep learning.

In summary, implementing PBL successfully requires careful planning, clear guidelines, collaboration, and reflection. By following these best practices and recommendations, educators can create a rich and meaningful learning experience for students, fostering their problem-solving abilities, critical thinking skills, and motivation to learn.

Section 3: Flipped Classroom Model

Overview of the Flipped Classroom Model

The flipped classroom model is a teaching approach that reverses the traditional order of learning activities. In a traditional classroom, students attend lectures in class and then complete homework assignments outside of class. However, in a flipped classroom, students are introduced to the content through self-paced instructional materials, such as pre-recorded videos or online resources, before coming to class. Class time is then used for collaborative and interactive activities, like discussions, problem-solving, and hands-on projects.

The flipped classroom model aims to enhance student engagement, promote active learning, and personalize the learning experience. It recognizes that students have different learning preferences and needs, and provides flexibility for students to learn at their own pace. By shifting the transmission of information from the teacher-led classroom to individual learning outside of class, educators can create more opportunities for deeper understanding and application of knowledge during in-person class time.

Benefits of the Flipped Classroom

The flipped classroom model offers several benefits for both students and teachers. Firstly, it allows students to take control of their learning and engage with the content at their own pace. Students can review the instructional materials multiple times, pause and rewind videos, and access additional resources to reinforce their understanding. This individualized learning approach promotes a deeper understanding of the concepts and improves retention.

Secondly, the flipped classroom increases student engagement and participation during class. As students come prepared with prior knowledge, the class time can be used for active learning activities that promote critical thinking, collaboration, and problem-solving skills. Students have the opportunity to ask questions, seek clarification, and engage in meaningful discussions with their peers and teachers.

Furthermore, the flipped classroom model promotes self-regulated learning and independent study skills. Students become responsible for managing their time, setting goals, and developing effective study strategies. They learn to take ownership of their learning process, which can enhance their long-term academic success.

Lastly, the flipped classroom provides teachers with more opportunities for individualized instruction and assessment. With the pre-recorded instructional materials, teachers can identify students' misconceptions and address them promptly during class. Teachers can also use class time to provide personalized feedback, monitor students' progress, and tailor instruction to meet individual learning needs.

Implementing the Flipped Classroom

To implement the flipped classroom model effectively, teachers need to carefully plan and design instructional materials. Here are some strategies for implementing the flipped classroom:

1. Identify learning objectives: Clearly define the learning outcomes that students should achieve and align them with the curriculum standards.

2. Select appropriate resources: Choose high-quality instructional materials that cater to different learning styles and preferences. These resources can include videos, articles, interactive simulations, or online quizzes.

3. Create engaging instructional videos: When creating instructional videos, teachers should keep them concise, well-structured, and visually appealing. Use multimedia elements like images, graphics, or animations to enhance understanding.

4. Provide additional learning resources: Supplement the instructional videos with supplementary resources, such as readings, practice exercises, or interactive online modules. This allows students to delve deeper into the topic and reinforce their understanding.

5. Communicate expectations and deadlines: Clearly communicate to students the expectations for watching the instructional videos and completing any accompanying activities. Provide deadlines and specific guidelines for class discussions or assignments.

6. Facilitate active learning activities: Plan interactive and engaging activities that encourage student participation and collaboration. These activities can include group discussions, debates, simulations, case studies, or hands-on experiments.

7. Assess student learning: Design formative and summative assessments to evaluate students' understanding and progress. Use a variety of assessment

methods, such as quizzes, projects, presentations, or reflective journals, to cater to diverse learning needs.

8. Provide timely feedback: Give students timely and constructive feedback on their performance to support their learning and growth. Feedback can be provided both during class activities and through online platforms.

Case Studies

The flipped classroom model has been successfully implemented in various educational settings across subjects and grade levels. Here are two case studies that showcase the effectiveness of the flipped classroom:

1. Mathematics: In a high school mathematics class, the teacher flipped the learning by providing instructional videos covering new concepts. Students were required to watch the videos outside of class and come prepared for class activities. During class time, students engaged in collaborative problem-solving activities, where they applied the concepts learned from the videos. This approach allowed students to develop a deeper understanding of mathematical concepts and improved their problem-solving skills.

2. Science: In an undergraduate biology course, the professor used the flipped classroom model to teach complex biological processes. Students were provided with pre-recorded video lectures and accompanying readings before each class. In-class activities focused on analyzing case studies, conducting experiments, and engaging in discussions. This approach facilitated a deeper understanding of the subject matter and allowed students to apply their knowledge to real-world scenarios.

These case studies demonstrate how the flipped classroom model can be adapted to different subjects and contexts to enhance student learning and engagement.

Challenges and Considerations

While the flipped classroom model offers numerous benefits, there are also challenges that educators may face during implementation. Here are some considerations to address these challenges:

1. Access to technology: Ensure that all students have access to the necessary technology and reliable internet connection to watch instructional videos and complete online activities. Provide alternatives for students who may not have access to technology, such as providing printed materials or offering computer lab facilities.

2.   Student accountability: Emphasize the importance of students' active engagement with the pre-class materials. Implement strategies to monitor and encourage student participation, such as online assessments or in-class discussions.

3. Time management: Help students develop time management skills to ensure they allocate sufficient time for watching videos, completing activities, and preparing for in-class discussions. Provide guidelines and reminders to help students stay on track.

4.   Teacher support and training: Offer professional development opportunities and support for teachers to effectively design and implement flipped classroom strategies. Collaboration and sharing of best practices among teachers can also enhance the success of the implementation.

5. Assessment alignment: Ensure that the assessments align with the learning outcomes and instructional materials. Design assessments that evaluate students' understanding and application of the concepts learned from both the instructional videos and in-class activities.

By considering these challenges and implementing strategies to address them, educators can maximize the benefits of the flipped classroom model and create a positive learning environment for their students.

Conclusion

The flipped classroom model provides an innovative and student-centered approach to teaching and learning. By leveraging technology and utilizing class time for interactive and collaborative activities, educators can enhance student engagement, promote deeper understanding, and personalize the learning experience. The flipped classroom model offers various benefits, including increased student participation, improved retention of knowledge, and the development of critical thinking skills. By carefully planning instructional materials, facilitating active learning activities, and providing timely feedback, teachers can successfully implement the flipped classroom model and create a more effective and engaging learning environment for their students.

Subsection 2: Strategies for preparing and delivering flipped lessons

In a flipped classroom model, the traditional approach of delivering instructional content in class and assigning practice or homework outside of class is reversed. In this section, we will explore effective strategies for preparing and delivering flipped lessons, ensuring that students engage with the content outside of the classroom and are ready for more interactive and collaborative activities during class time.

To successfully implement the flipped classroom model, teachers need to carefully plan and design their lessons. Here are some strategies to consider:

1. Preparing Video Lectures: - Use concise and engaging videos: Keep your videos short (around 5-10 minutes) and break them down into smaller, focused topics.   Use visuals, animations, and real-life examples to enhance student understanding and interest. - Maintain a conversational tone: Speak directly to the camera as if you are having a one-on-one conversation with the students. This helps create a sense of connection and makes the content more relatable. - Provide clear explanations and examples: Use simple language, avoid jargon, and provide concrete examples to help students grasp difficult concepts.   - Incorporate formative assessments: Embed formative assessment questions throughout the video to check for understanding and provide immediate feedback to students.

2. Providing Supplemental Resources: - Curate resources: Identify additional readings, online articles, interactive simulations, or tutorials to supplement the video lectures. These resources should deepen students' understanding of the topic and cater to different learning preferences. - Create study guides or summaries: Provide students with study guides or summaries that highlight the key points from the video lectures and supplemental resources. This will help students focus on the most important information.

3. Engaging Students Outside the Classroom: - Assign pre-class activities: Design activities that require students to engage with the instructional content before coming to class. For example, you can ask them to complete quizzes, write short reflections, or solve problems related to the video lectures and supplemental resources. - Foster online discussions: Use online platforms or discussion boards to encourage students to ask questions, share insights, and collaborate with their peers. This creates a sense of community and allows students to learn from each other.

4. Facilitating In-Class Activities: - Focus on application and problem-solving: In class, engage students in activities that apply the knowledge they have gained through the pre-class work. Encourage problem-solving, critical thinking, and group collaboration. - Provide guidance and feedback: Act as a facilitator and guide during in-class activities. Offer support and feedback to students as they work through problems or complete projects. This personalized attention enhances the learning experience.

5. Assessing Learning: - Use formative assessments: Throughout the flipped lesson, employ formative assessments to gauge student understanding. This can include quizzes, exit tickets, or short assignments. - Incorporate summative

assessments: At the end of a unit or lesson, use summative assessments to evaluate student learning. These can be traditional exams, projects, or presentations.

It's important to remember that the flipped classroom model is not a one-size-fits-all approach. Teachers should adapt and modify these strategies based on their students' needs and the specific subject matter. Flexibility and continuous reflection on the effectiveness of the flipped model are key.

In addition to the strategies mentioned above, here are a few tips and tricks to enhance the effectiveness of flipped lessons:

- Solicit student feedback: Regularly ask students for feedback on the flipped lessons. This feedback can help identify areas for improvement and adjust the instructional approach accordingly. - Promote active learning: Encourage students to actively engage with the videos and supplemental resources by taking notes, pausing to reflect, or answering the embedded questions. This helps enhance their comprehension and retention of the material. - Use data to inform instruction: Utilize data collected from formative and summative assessments to inform your instructional decisions. Analyze the results to identify common misconceptions or areas where additional support may be needed.

Remember, effective implementation of flipped lessons requires careful planning, ongoing reflection, and a commitment to student-centered learning. By incorporating these strategies and personalizing the learning experience, you can create an engaging and dynamic flipped classroom environment.

For more in-depth information and examples of successful implementation of the flipped classroom model, you can refer to the following resources:

- Bergmann, J., & Sams, A. (2012). Flip your classroom: Reach every student in every class every day. International Society for Technology in Education. - Tucker, B. (2012). The flipped classroom. Education Next, 12(1), 82-83. - Bergmann, J., Overmyer, J., & Wilie, B. (2018). The flipped learning toolkit: A practical guide to flipping your classroom. International Society for Technology in Education.

Now that we have explored strategies for preparing and delivering flipped lessons, let's move on to the next section, where we will discuss addressing challenges and maximizing the benefits of the flipped classroom model.

Subsection 3: Case studies of successful implementation of the flipped classroom model

In this subsection, we will explore real-life case studies of successful implementation of the flipped classroom model. These case studies will provide insights into the various ways teachers have applied the flipped classroom approach and the positive impact it has had on student learning outcomes. We will examine different grade levels and subject areas to showcase the versatility of the flipped classroom model.

Case Study 1: Flipped Math Classroom in Elementary School

Mrs. Johnson, a 4th-grade math teacher at Lincoln Elementary School, wanted to find a way to engage her students more actively in class and improve their understanding of mathematical concepts. She decided to implement the flipped classroom model.

Mrs. Johnson recorded short tutorial videos, explaining key math concepts and problem-solving strategies, and made them available to her students before each class. The students were required to watch the videos at home and come to class prepared with questions and areas where they needed clarification.

During class time, Mrs. Johnson engaged the students in hands-on activities and problem-solving exercises related to the video lessons. The students worked collaboratively, discussing their ideas and applying the concepts they had learned. Mrs. Johnson provided individualized support, addressing specific misconceptions and guiding students through challenging problems.

The flipped classroom approach allowed Mrs. Johnson to maximize classroom time for active learning and individualized instruction. The students reported feeling more confident in their math skills and enjoyed the interactive activities during class. The flipped classroom model also fostered a sense of responsibility and ownership in their learning.

Case Study 2: Flipped Science Classroom in High School

Mr. Rodriguez, a high school biology teacher at Greenfield High, wanted to create a more dynamic and interactive learning environment for his students. He decided to implement the flipped classroom model in his biology class.

Mr. Rodriguez selected videos and online resources that covered the content for each lesson and posted them on the class website. Before coming to class, students were required to watch the videos and complete online quizzes to check their understanding. This allowed them to familiarize themselves with the concepts and terminology before engaging in hands-on activities during class.

In the classroom, Mr. Rodriguez facilitated collaborative discussions and conducted experiments related to the topics covered in the videos. He used concept maps and graphic organizers to help students visualize the connections between different biological concepts. Students actively participated in group projects, research assignments, and presentations, applying their knowledge to real-world scenarios.

The flipped classroom model transformed the learning experience for Mr. Rodriguez's students. They developed a deeper understanding of biology concepts, improved their critical thinking skills, and became more confident in their abilities to conduct scientific investigations. The interactive nature of the flipped classroom model fostered a love for science and motivated students to pursue further studies in the field.

Case Study 3: Flipped Language Classroom in Middle School

Ms. Lee, a middle school Spanish teacher at Westwood Middle School, wanted to create a more immersive language learning experience for her students. She decided to implement the flipped classroom model in her Spanish class.

Ms. Lee recorded videos of herself speaking in Spanish, introducing vocabulary, grammar rules, and phrases commonly used in everyday conversations. She uploaded these videos to a video-sharing platform, along with supplemental materials such as worksheets and interactive quizzes.

Students were required to watch the videos and complete the associated activities at home. During class time, Ms. Lee facilitated immersive language activities, such as role-playing, dialogues, and cultural discussions. Students practiced speaking and listening to Spanish in pairs or small groups, applying the vocabulary and grammar they had learned from the videos.

The flipped classroom model provided students with more opportunities for interaction and practice in the target language. They became more confident in their ability to communicate in Spanish and developed a deeper appreciation for the language and culture. The interactive and communicative activities in the classroom improved their language proficiency and prepared them for real-life language use.

Summary

In this subsection, we explored three case studies that highlight the successful implementation of the flipped classroom model in different grade levels and subject areas. These case studies demonstrated the positive impact of the flipped classroom approach on student engagement, understanding, and learning outcomes.

The flipped classroom model, as showcased in these case studies, allows for a more personalized and active learning experience. By shifting the traditional lecture to outside of class, teachers can maximize classroom time for student-centered activities, collaborative learning, and individualized instruction. The flipped classroom model also empowers students to take ownership of their learning and prepares them for the challenges of the modern world.

While these case studies illustrate the benefits of the flipped classroom model, it is important to note that successful implementation requires careful planning, ongoing assessment, and flexibility to meet the needs of diverse learners. Teachers need to adapt the flipped classroom approach to their specific contexts and continuously reflect on its effectiveness.

By embracing the flipped classroom model, educators can create transformative learning experiences that empower students and prepare them for success in the 21st-century world.

Subsection 4: Addressing challenges and maximizing the benefits of the flipped classroom

The flipped classroom model has gained popularity in recent years for its potential to enhance student engagement, promote active learning, and personalize instruction. However, like any educational approach, it is not without its challenges. In this section, we will explore some of the common challenges faced when implementing the flipped classroom model and strategies to address them. We will also discuss how to maximize the benefits of this approach in order to create an effective learning environment.

One of the main challenges in the flipped classroom model is ensuring that students come prepared for in-class activities. As students are expected to engage with instructional materials outside of the classroom, there is a risk that some may not take the necessary time to review the content. To address this challenge, instructors can consider the following strategies:

1.   Clear Expectations and Communication: Clearly communicate the expectations for out-of-class preparation to students from the beginning. Emphasize the importance of reviewing the content before coming to class and explain how it will contribute to their learning experience. Regularly remind students of upcoming topics and provide them with guidelines for effective pre-class preparation.

2. Varied Pre-Class Materials: Provide a variety of pre-class materials such as videos, readings, interactive online modules, or quizzes. This helps cater to different learning styles and preferences, increasing the likelihood that students will engage with the content. Additionally, encourage students to share their preferred resources or suggest alternative ones that may better suit their learning needs.

3. Accountability Measures: Implement accountability measures to ensure that students are completing the pre-class activities. This can be done through quizzes, online discussions, or reflective journals. By holding students accountable for their learning, they will be more likely to come to class prepared.

Another challenge in the flipped classroom model is managing the in-class activities effectively. With limited time in face-to-face sessions, instructors need to create opportunities for active learning and student interaction. Here are some strategies to address this challenge:

1. Thoughtful Activity Design: Design in-class activities that require higher-order thinking and promote collaborative and critical thinking skills. Encourage students to engage in problem-solving, case studies, debates, or group projects. These activities make the most of the face-to-face time and provide opportunities for students to apply and deepen their understanding of the content.

2. Facilitation and Guidance: As the instructor, take on the role of a facilitator and guide students through the in-class activities. Ensure that everyone is actively participating and offer support when needed. Facilitate discussions, ask probing questions, and provide timely feedback to foster deeper learning and reflection.

3. Flexible Grouping: Use flexible grouping strategies to promote collaboration and diversity of perspectives. Allow students to work in pairs, small groups, or larger groups based on the nature of the activity. Encourage them to share their knowledge, learn from each other, and collectively solve problems.

Finally, maximizing the benefits of the flipped classroom model requires ongoing reflection and revision. Continuous improvement is essential for optimizing student learning and engagement. Consider the following strategies:

1. Regular Feedback: Seek feedback from students regarding their experience with the flipped model. Ask for their input on the clarity of pre-class materials, the effectiveness of in-class activities, and their overall satisfaction with the approach. Use this feedback to refine and improve your instructional practices.

2. Continuous Professional Development: Engage in professional development opportunities focused on flipped learning. Attend workshops, webinars, or conferences to stay updated on the latest research and best practices. Connect with other educators who are implementing the flipped classroom model to share ideas, resources, and lessons learned.

3. Flexibility and Adaptability: Be open to adjusting your instructional practices based on student needs and feedback. Flexibility is key when implementing the flipped classroom model, as it allows you to adapt the approach to the specific learning goals and preferences of your students.

In conclusion, the flipped classroom model offers numerous benefits for both teachers and learners. However, it is important to address the challenges that may arise during implementation.   By setting clear expectations, implementing accountability measures, designing thoughtful in-class activities, and continuously reflecting on the effectiveness of the approach, educators can maximize the benefits of the flipped classroom and create an engaging and student-centered learning environment.

Note: *The strategies and recommendations provided in this section are based on educational research and best practices. However, it is important to remember that each classroom and context is unique. Educators should adapt these strategies to meet the specific needs and goals of their students.*

Subsection 5: Exploring alternative models of flipped learning

In the previous subsections, we discussed the fundamentals of the flipped classroom model, strategies for implementing it, and successful case studies. However, the field of education is constantly evolving, and educators are always seeking new approaches to enhance student engagement and learning. In this subsection, we will explore alternative models of flipped learning that offer innovative ways to deliver content and promote active learning.

One alternative model of flipped learning is the Station Rotation model. In this model, students rotate through various learning stations, each offering a different learning activity. One station may involve working on an online module, another may have group discussions or collaborative projects, and another may provide one-on-one teacher instruction. This model allows for personalized learning experiences and accommodates varying learning styles. It also fosters student autonomy and promotes collaboration among peers.

Another emerging model is the Peer Instruction model. This model emphasizes peer-to-peer interaction and active learning. Students take on the role of both learners and educators, engaging in discussions and explaining concepts to their peers. The instructor acts as a facilitator, guiding the discussions and addressing any misconceptions. Peer Instruction promotes deeper conceptual understanding, critical thinking, and metacognitive skills. It also creates a supportive and collaborative learning environment.

A flipped mastery model is another alternative that focuses on individualized learning and competency-based progression. In this model, students advance at their own pace, mastering the content before moving on to the next level. The instructor provides resources and supports, such as video lectures and practice exercises, which students engage with outside of class. Class time is then devoted to applying knowledge, problem-solving, and receiving personalized feedback.

Flipped mastery enhances student ownership of learning, allows for differentiated instruction, and ensures a deep understanding of concepts.

One unconventional approach is the Gamified Flipped Classroom model. This model incorporates elements of gamification into the flipped classroom structure, aiming to increase motivation and engagement. Students earn points, badges, or rewards for completing tasks, mastering concepts, and participating in class activities. The instructor can use technology platforms or game-based learning systems to deliver content and track progress. Gamified flipped learning can make the learning process enjoyable, immersive, and competitive, fostering a sense of achievement and mastery.

It's important to note that these alternative models of flipped learning are not mutually exclusive, and they can be combined or adapted to suit specific educational contexts and objectives. Educators should carefully consider the needs and preferences of their students when exploring alternative models. Furthermore, implementing these models requires thoughtful planning and resource allocation.

In order to successfully implement alternative models of flipped learning, educators should consider the following:

1. Set clear learning objectives: Clearly define the learning outcomes and expectations for students in each model.

2. Provide necessary resources: Ensure access to technology, online modules, and other materials required for the alternative models.

3. Training and support: Offer professional development opportunities and ongoing support for educators to familiarize themselves with the alternative models and effectively implement them.

4. Assessment and feedback: Design appropriate assessment strategies aligned with the alternative models and provide timely feedback to students to guide their learning.

5. Continuous evaluation and improvement: Regularly evaluate the effectiveness of the alternative models and make necessary adjustments based on student feedback and outcomes.

By exploring and implementing alternative models of flipped learning, educators can tap into students' diverse learning preferences, promote active engagement, and enhance learning outcomes. These models offer exciting opportunities to transform the traditional classroom and create dynamic and student-centered learning environments.

Example: Applying the Station Rotation Model

Let's take a look at an example of how the Station Rotation model can be applied in a high school biology class.

In this scenario, the teacher divides the class into three groups and sets up three stations. The first station is a computer lab, where students engage with online modules and interactive simulations related to the topic of genetics. They can explore genetics concepts at their own pace and access additional resources as needed.

The second station is a small group discussion station. Here, students work collaboratively to solve genetics problems and discuss their understanding of the topic. The teacher provides guiding questions and monitors the discussions to ensure that students are on track.

The third station is a teacher-led instruction station. The teacher provides targeted instruction on complex genetics concepts and answers any questions that students may have. This station allows for individualized support and clarification.

Students rotate through the three stations, spending equal time at each. By the end of the class period, all students have engaged in independent online learning, collaborative problem-solving, and direct instruction.

This Station Rotation model provides a balanced approach, incorporating technology-enhanced learning, peer interaction, and personalized instruction. It allows students to explore genetics from different perspectives and engage in hands-on activities. The model not only promotes active learning but also fosters a deeper understanding of genetics concepts.

Chapter 2: Practical Strategies for Effective Teaching and Learning

Section 1: Classroom Management

Subsection 1: Establishing an Inclusive and Positive Classroom Environment

Creating an inclusive and positive classroom environment is essential for promoting student engagement, fostering a sense of belonging, and enhancing learning outcomes. In this subsection, we will explore strategies and practices that teachers can implement to establish such an environment.

Understanding Inclusion in the Classroom

Inclusion in the classroom refers to the practice of providing equal opportunities for all students, regardless of their abilities, backgrounds, or identities. It involves creating a supportive and accepting environment where every student feels valued, respected, and included.

To establish inclusivity, teachers should:

1. Recognize and celebrate diversity: Embrace the uniqueness of each student and create a culture that values diversity in terms of race, ethnicity, gender, socioeconomic status, religion, abilities, and learning styles.

2. Foster a sense of belonging: Develop strong relationships with students and among students themselves. Encourage collaboration, teamwork, and mutual support to create a sense of community within the classroom.

3. Promote empathy and understanding: Teach students to appreciate and respect different perspectives and experiences. Facilitate discussions on inclusion and social justice to enhance students' empathy and understanding of others.

4. Use inclusive language and materials: Be mindful of the language used in the classroom and ensure that it promotes inclusivity. Incorporate diverse perspectives in instructional materials, including textbooks and literature, to reflect the experiences of all students.

Positive Classroom Management Strategies

Positive classroom management involves creating a structured and supportive environment that promotes positive behavior, engagement, and learning. When students feel safe and supported, they are more likely to participate actively and achieve their full potential.

Here are some strategies for establishing a positive classroom environment:

1. Establish clear expectations: Set and communicate clear guidelines and expectations for behavior, academic performance, and classroom routines. This helps students understand what is expected of them and promotes a sense of structure and predictability.

2. Reinforce positive behavior: Recognize and reinforce positive behavior through verbal praise, rewards, or a system of incentives. This encourages students to make positive choices and motivates them to actively engage in learning.

3. Build positive relationships: Develop positive and respectful relationships with each student. Take the time to get to know their interests, strengths, and challenges. Show genuine care and concern for their well-being, both academically and personally.

4. Use effective communication: Maintain open and honest communication with students. Be approachable and listen actively to their concerns. Provide constructive feedback and guidance to help students grow and improve.

5. Address conflicts promptly: Actively address conflicts or disruptive behavior in a fair and respectful manner. Encourage peaceful resolution strategies such as open dialogue, negotiation, and compromise. Teach students conflict resolution skills to promote a harmonious classroom environment.

Creating an Inclusive Learning Environment

Inclusive learning environments enable every student to access and engage with the curriculum effectively. To create such an environment, teachers can implement the following strategies:

1. Differentiate instruction: Recognize and accommodate different learning styles, abilities, and needs of students. Provide varying levels of support, resources, and materials to ensure that all students can access the curriculum and succeed.

2. Encourage student collaboration: Promote collaborative learning activities that encourage students to work together, share ideas, and support one another. Create opportunities for peer tutoring, group projects, and cooperative learning to foster a sense of teamwork and inclusivity.

3. Use universal design principles: Incorporate universal design principles when planning lessons and creating learning materials. This involves designing instruction and resources that are accessible and usable by all students, regardless of their abilities or disabilities.

4. Provide assistive technologies and aids: Use technology tools, assistive devices, and aids that help students with disabilities or learning challenges fully participate in the learning process. Ensure that students are aware of and have access to available support resources.

5. Regularly assess and adapt instruction: Monitor student progress through formative assessments and adjust instruction accordingly. Provide timely and specific feedback to guide students' learning and address individual needs.

Example: Promoting Inclusivity Through Cooperative Learning

Cooperative learning is an effective strategy for promoting inclusivity in the classroom. It encourages students to work together towards a common goal, fostering collaboration, communication, and mutual support.

For example, in a science class, students could be divided into diverse groups and assigned a complex experiment that requires teamwork. Each group member would have a specific role and responsibility to ensure the success of the experiment. Students would need to communicate, share ideas, and support one another throughout the process.

This cooperative learning activity allows students to appreciate the diversity of their team members, utilize each member's strengths, and develop important social and problem-solving skills. Through such collaborative experiences, students learn to appreciate and value the contributions of individuals from different backgrounds, promoting a truly inclusive classroom environment.

Additional Resources

- Teaching Tolerance: `https://www.tolerance.org/`

- National Education Association - Inclusive Classroom Strategies: `https://www.nea.org/resources-tools/teaching-inclusive-classroom`

- CAST: Universal Design for Learning: `http://www.cast.org/our-work/about-udl.html`

- Teaching Channel: Creating an Inclusive Classroom: `https://www.teachingchannel.com/video/inclusion-strategies`

In conclusion, establishing an inclusive and positive classroom environment is crucial for maximizing student learning and well-being. By embracing diversity, using positive classroom management strategies, and creating inclusive learning experiences, teachers can create an environment where all students feel valued, respected, and motivated to succeed.

Subsection 2: Effective Strategies for Behavior Management

Effective behavior management is essential for creating a positive and productive learning environment. It involves implementing strategies that promote discipline, engagement, and cooperation among students. In this subsection, we will explore various strategies that are known to be effective in managing classroom behavior.

Establishing Clear Expectations and Rules

The first step in behavior management is to establish clear expectations and rules for classroom behavior. This provides students with a clear understanding of what is expected from them and helps create a sense of structure. When developing expectations and rules, it is important to involve students in the process to ensure a sense of ownership and understanding.

One effective strategy is to create a set of positively phrased rules that outline expected behaviors. For example, instead of saying "No talking during class," a rule could be phrased as "Respect others' need for quiet during class activities." This positive phrasing helps students understand the desired behavior and promotes a more positive and respectful classroom environment.

Positive Reinforcement

Positive reinforcement is a powerful tool for behavior management. It involves providing praise, rewards, or other positive consequences for desired behaviors. By reinforcing positive behaviors, students are more likely to repeat them in the future. This strategy helps create a positive and supportive classroom environment.

One effective method of positive reinforcement is to use a system of rewards. This can include verbal praise, stickers, tokens, or a points system. For example, students can earn points for following classroom rules, completing assignments on time, or demonstrating good behavior. These points can then be exchanged for small rewards or privileges, such as extra free time or a special classroom privilege.

It is important to remember that positive reinforcement should be specific and immediate. Recognize and reinforce desired behaviors as soon as possible to make the connection between the behavior and the reward clear.

Clear and Consistent Consequences

In addition to positive reinforcement, it is equally important to establish clear and consistent consequences for inappropriate behavior. Consistency helps students understand the consequences of their actions and promotes a sense of fairness.

When implementing consequences, it is crucial to ensure that they are reasonable, age-appropriate, and related to the behavior. Consequences should also be clearly communicated to students in advance so they understand the potential outcomes of their actions. Some common consequences include verbal warnings, loss of privileges, time-outs, or parent-teacher conferences.

It is important to note that consequences should be used as a teaching tool, rather than a form of punishment. They should aim to help students reflect on their behavior, develop self-control, and make better choices in the future.

Effective Communication

Effective communication plays a vital role in behavior management. Building strong relationships with students allows for open and respectful communication, which can help prevent and resolve behavior issues.

To promote effective communication, teachers should create an environment where students feel comfortable expressing their thoughts and concerns. Active listening is an essential part of effective communication. Teachers should actively listen to students, validate their feelings, and respond empathetically.

Additionally, clear and concise instructions can help minimize misunderstandings and confusion. Teachers should provide instructions in a step-by-step manner, using simple and straightforward language. Visual aids, such as diagrams or charts, can also be helpful in reinforcing verbal instructions.

Classroom Routines and Procedures

Establishing clear routines and procedures is another effective strategy for behavior management. Routines provide students with structure and predictability, reducing the likelihood of disruptive behavior.

Teachers should establish routines for daily activities, such as entering the classroom, transitioning between subjects, and packing up at the end of the day. Clear procedures should be communicated to students and consistently reinforced. For example, a routine for entering the classroom could include students hanging up their coats, putting their backpacks away, and starting a warm-up activity.

It is important to provide explicit instruction and practice for each routine and procedure at the beginning of the school year. Reinforce these routines regularly to ensure students internalize them.

Problem-Solving and Conflict Resolution

Teaching students problem-solving and conflict resolution skills empowers them to resolve conflicts and manage their own behavior. These skills help create a positive and respectful classroom environment where students can effectively communicate and work together.

Teachers can teach problem-solving skills by outlining a step-by-step process for identifying and finding solutions to conflicts. This process can include steps such as defining the problem, brainstorming possible solutions, evaluating the pros and cons, and selecting the best solution.

Conflict resolution skills can be taught through role-plays or structured group discussions. Encourage students to actively listen to each other, express their feelings, and find mutually beneficial solutions.

Building Relationships and a Positive Classroom Culture

Building positive relationships with students is essential for effective behavior management. When students trust and respect their teacher, they are more likely to exhibit positive behavior and engage in the learning process.

Teachers can foster positive relationships by getting to know their students on an individual level. Take an interest in their lives, hobbies, and interests. Show genuine care and concern for their well-being.

Creating a positive classroom culture is also important. This involves celebrating student achievements, promoting collaboration and teamwork, and creating opportunities for students to take on leadership roles. A positive and inclusive classroom culture encourages students to be their best selves.

Cultural Sensitivity and Equity

Behavior management strategies should be culturally sensitive and promote equity among students. Teachers should be mindful of their own biases and create an environment that respects and values students from all cultural backgrounds.

Tailor behavior management strategies to reflect the cultural diversity of the classroom. Take into consideration cultural norms, values, and communication styles. Provide opportunities for students to share and celebrate their cultural heritage.

Promote equity by treating all students fairly and addressing individual needs. Be mindful of systemic biases that may disproportionately affect certain groups of students. Provide additional support and resources to ensure all students have an equal opportunity to succeed.

Conclusion

Effective behavior management is crucial for creating a positive and productive learning environment. By implementing strategies such as establishing clear expectations and rules, using positive reinforcement, providing clear and consistent consequences, promoting effective communication, establishing classroom routines and procedures, teaching problem-solving and conflict resolution skills, building relationships, and fostering a positive classroom culture, educators can create a classroom environment conducive to learning and growth. Remember, every classroom is unique, so it is important to continually reflect on these strategies and adapt them to meet the individual needs of your students.

Subsection 3: Promoting Student Engagement and Motivation

Engaging and motivating students is crucial for creating a positive learning environment and fostering academic success. When students are actively engaged in their education and motivated to learn, they are more likely to retain information, participate in class discussions, and apply what they have learned in real-life situations. In this section, we will explore various strategies to promote student engagement and motivation in the classroom.

Understanding Student Engagement

Before discussing strategies to promote engagement, it is important to understand what student engagement entails. Student engagement refers to the level of attention, interest, and involvement that students demonstrate in their learning. It goes beyond mere compliance with classroom rules or passive listening. Engaged students are enthusiastic about their learning, actively participate in class activities, and connect their learning to real-world contexts.

Creating a Positive Classroom Climate

One of the foundational elements for promoting student engagement and motivation is creating a positive classroom climate. A positive classroom climate fosters a sense of belonging and encourages students to take risks, ask questions, and contribute to discussions. Here are some strategies to create a positive classroom climate:

- **Build positive relationships:** Get to know your students individually, show interest in their lives, and create a safe and respectful environment where they feel comfortable expressing their thoughts and opinions.

- **Celebrate diversity:** Embrace the uniqueness of each student and create a classroom environment that values and appreciates diversity. Encourage students to share their cultural experiences and perspectives to enrich the learning environment.

- **Establish clear expectations:** Set clear and reasonable expectations for behavior and academic performance. Communicate these expectations clearly and consistently, and provide guidance and support to help students meet them.

Active Learning Strategies

Active learning strategies involve engaging students directly in the learning process, encouraging them to think critically, solve problems, and apply concepts. Here are some effective active learning strategies to promote student engagement:

+ **Group discussions:** Assign students to small groups and provide them with thought-provoking questions or problems to discuss. Encourage active participation, collaboration, and respectful dialogue among group members.

+ **Problem-based learning:** Present students with real-life problems or scenarios related to the subject matter. Guide them through the process of investigating, analyzing, and proposing solutions to these problems. This approach helps students see the relevance of what they are learning and enhances their critical thinking skills.

+ **Hands-on activities:** Incorporate hands-on activities, experiments, and simulations that allow students to actively engage with the content and apply their knowledge. These activities make learning more interactive and memorable.

+ **Role-playing or simulations:** Assign roles to students and have them act out scenarios or participate in simulated experiences related to the topic of study. This approach promotes active engagement and helps students develop empathy and problem-solving skills.

Technology Integration

Incorporating technology into teaching and learning can significantly enhance student engagement and motivation. Here are some ways to integrate technology effectively:

+ **Interactive presentations:** Use multimedia tools to create interactive presentations that captivate students' attention and make learning visually appealing and interactive.

+ **Online discussions and collaboration:** Utilize online platforms or discussion boards to facilitate student discussions, collaboration, and peer feedback. This allows students to participate in academic conversations beyond the classroom walls.

+ **Digital storytelling:** Engage students in creating digital stories or presentations to showcase their understanding of concepts. This creative approach integrates technology while giving students a platform to demonstrate their knowledge.

+ **Gamification:** Introduce game-like elements such as point systems, levels, and rewards to make learning more engaging and enjoyable. Gamification can motivate students to actively participate and strive for academic success.

Building Autonomy and Relevance

Students are more likely to be engaged and motivated when they feel a sense of autonomy and relevance in their learning. Here are some strategies to promote autonomy and relevance:

+ **Choice and autonomy:** Provide students with choices in assignments, project topics, or problem-solving approaches. This fosters a sense of ownership and empowers students to take responsibility for their learning.

+ **Real-world connections:** Connect the content to real-world contexts, current events, or students' personal experiences. Demonstrating the relevance of what they are learning helps students see the practical applications and importance of their education.

+ **Goal-setting and progress monitoring:** Collaborate with students to set individual learning goals and regularly assess their progress. This process enables students to track their achievements and take ownership of their learning journey.

Encouraging Intrinsic Motivation

Intrinsic motivation refers to the internal drive and desire to engage in an activity for its inherent satisfaction or personal interest. Cultivating intrinsic motivation is essential for long-term engagement and academic success. Here are some strategies to encourage intrinsic motivation:

+ **Offer praise and recognition:** Recognize students' efforts, achievements, and growth, both publicly and privately. Provide specific feedback that highlights their strengths and encourages further improvement.

+ **Foster a growth mindset:** Teach students about the power of a growth mindset and the belief that intelligence and abilities can be developed through effort and practice. Encourage students to embrace challenges, persist in the face of setbacks, and view mistakes as opportunities for learning and growth.

+ **Tap into student interests:** Incorporate students' interests and passions into the curriculum whenever possible. This helps create a personal connection to the content and enhances engagement and motivation.

Addressing Barriers to Engagement and Motivation

Despite our best efforts, some students may still face barriers to engagement and motivation. It is important to identify and address these barriers to ensure all students have an equal opportunity to succeed. Here are some common barriers and potential strategies to overcome them:

+ **Lack of relevance:** Ensure the content is meaningful and applicable to students' lives. Provide examples and illustrations that resonate with their experiences and cultural backgrounds.

+ **Negative peer influences:** Foster a positive classroom culture that discourages negative peer influences and supports constructive collaboration. Encourage students to be supportive, respectful, and inclusive of their peers.

+ **Learning difficulties or disabilities:** Differentiate instruction and provide appropriate support to students with learning difficulties or disabilities. Use varied instructional methods and resources to accommodate diverse learning needs.

+ **External distractions:** Minimize external distractions such as noise or disruptions in the classroom environment. Create a calm and focused atmosphere that allows students to concentrate on their learning.

Conclusion

Promoting student engagement and motivation is a continuous process that requires intentional strategies and an understanding of students' needs and interests. By creating a positive classroom climate, implementing active learning strategies, integrating technology effectively, and fostering autonomy and relevance, educators can inspire students to become active, lifelong learners. Remember that every student is unique, and it may take time and experimentation to find the most effective strategies for promoting engagement and motivation in your specific classroom. Embrace flexibility, always be open to feedback, and continuously adapt your practices to meet the evolving needs of your students.

Subsection 4: Addressing Individual Needs and Learning Differences in the Classroom

In any classroom, students come with unique backgrounds, skills, and learning styles. As educators, it is vital to recognize and address the individual needs and learning differences of our students to create an inclusive and effective learning environment. This subsection explores strategies and approaches that can help teachers cater to the diverse needs of their students.

Understanding Individual Needs and Learning Differences

Every student has different strengths, weaknesses, and preferred ways of learning. Some students may excel in visual learning, while others may grasp concepts better through auditory or kinesthetic means. Additionally, some students may have learning disabilities or special educational needs that require additional support.

To effectively address individual needs, teachers should:

- Get to know their students: Take the time to learn about each student's background, interests, and learning styles. Building personal connections with students can help create a positive learning environment and enable teachers to tailor their instruction accordingly.

- Use diagnostic assessments: Regularly assess students' learning styles, preferences, and skill levels using diagnostic assessments. These assessments provide valuable insights into individual needs and help teachers customize their teaching strategies accordingly.

- Collaborate with support teams: Work closely with special education teachers, counselors, and other support staff to identify students who require additional assistance. Collaboration ensures that students receive the support they need to succeed academically and socially.

Differentiating Instruction

Once teachers have a clear understanding of their students' individual needs, they can employ differentiated instruction strategies to address those needs effectively.

Differentiated instruction involves tailoring teaching methods, materials, and assessments to accommodate diverse learning styles and skill levels within a single classroom.

Here are some strategies for differentiating instruction:

+ Flexible grouping: Organize students into small groups based on their learning needs and abilities. This allows teachers to deliver targeted instruction and provide appropriate challenges to each group.

+ Varied instructional materials: Provide students with a range of resources, such as textbooks, articles, videos, and interactive online tools, to cater to different learning preferences. Offering multiple modalities helps students engage with the content in ways that suit their learning style.

+ Individualized learning plans: Develop individualized learning plans (ILPs) for students with special educational needs or specific learning goals. ILPs outline personalized goals, instructional strategies, and support interventions to ensure students receive the necessary assistance.

+ Tiered assignments: Create tiered assignments that scaffold learning and provide varying levels of challenge. Students can choose assignments that match their skill level, allowing for differentiation within the same task or project.

Promoting Inclusion and Collaboration

Creating an inclusive learning environment where students feel valued and supported is key to addressing individual needs. Inclusion goes beyond accommodating learning differences and extends to fostering a sense of belonging and acceptance for all students.

Here are some strategies to promote inclusion and collaboration:

+ Encourage peer support and collaboration: Foster a classroom culture that celebrates collaboration and teamwork. Encourage students to work in pairs or groups, allowing them to learn from and support one another.

+ Implement Universal Design for Learning (UDL) principles: UDL involves designing flexible learning environments that can be accessed by all students, regardless of their learning differences. By employing UDL principles, teachers can provide multiple means of representation, expression, and engagement, ensuring that instruction caters to diverse learners.

+ Create inclusive classroom routines: Establish classroom routines that cater to students' individual needs. For example, allow students extra time for assignments or provide alternative modes of assessment to accommodate different learning styles.

+ Foster a growth mindset: Encourage students to embrace a growth mindset by emphasizing effort, resilience, and ongoing improvement. Help students understand that everyone has unique learning paths and that mistakes and challenges are opportunities for growth.

While addressing individual needs and learning differences can present challenges, it is crucial for creating an inclusive and effective learning environment. By understanding students' unique strengths and employing appropriate strategies, educators can support the diverse needs of their learners and promote academic success for all.

Real-World Example: Differentiating Instruction in a Mathematics Classroom

Imagine a mathematics classroom where students have different levels of mathematical proficiency and learning styles. The teacher wants to differentiate instruction to ensure all students are appropriately challenged and supported.

The teacher may:

+ Use flexible grouping: Recognizing that some students learn best in cooperative settings, the teacher assigns group projects that allow students to work together. Other students who prefer independent work are assigned individual tasks that align with their skill level.

+ Provide varied instructional materials: The teacher offers a range of resources, including textbooks, online tutorials, and manipulatives, to cater to different learning preferences. Visual learners can access instructional videos, while kinesthetic learners can work with manipulatives during problem-solving activities.

+ Offer tiered assignments: The teacher designs assignments with varying levels of difficulty. Students with advanced mathematical skills can tackle more complex problems, while those who need extra support focus on foundational concepts.

+ Collaborate with special educators: The teacher collaborates with special education teachers to identify students who require additional assistance. Together, they develop individualized learning plans and provide necessary accommodations, such as extended time or assistive technology.

By implementing these strategies, the teacher addresses the diverse needs and learning differences in the classroom, ensuring that all students can actively engage in meaningful mathematics learning.

Additional Resources

+ Books:

  - "The Differentiated Classroom: Responding to the Needs of All Learners" by Carol Ann Tomlinson

  - "How to Differentiate Instruction in Academically Diverse Classrooms" by Carol Ann Tomlinson

  - "Universal Design for Learning: Theory and Practice" by Anne Meyer, David H. Rose, and David Gordon

+ Websites:

  - National Center on Universal Design for Learning: http://www.udlcenter.org

  - Teaching Tolerance: https://www.tolerance.org

  - Edutopia: https://www.edutopia.org

By implementing a variety of strategies, teachers can create an inclusive and supportive learning environment that addresses individual needs and learning differences. Differentiating instruction, promoting collaboration, and fostering a growth mindset are crucial steps toward ensuring that every student can thrive academically and personally.

Subsection 5: Preventing and Managing Conflicts in the Classroom

Conflict management is an essential skill for teachers to create a positive and productive learning environment. In this subsection, we will explore practical strategies for preventing and managing conflicts in the classroom. We'll discuss the importance of proactive measures, effective communication techniques, and the role of a supportive classroom culture in conflict resolution. We'll also examine common challenges in conflict management and provide appropriate solutions.

Proactive Measures to Prevent Conflict

Preventing conflicts before they arise is crucial for maintaining a harmonious classroom. Here are some proactive measures teachers can take:

+ **Establish clear rules and expectations:** Create a set of classroom rules with input from students, and ensure that everyone understands and agrees to follow them. Clearly communicate your expectations for behavior, respect, and cooperation.

+ **Promote a positive classroom culture:** Foster a supportive and inclusive classroom environment where students feel valued and respected. Encourage teamwork, empathy, and kindness among students. By establishing positive relationships and a strong sense of community, you can minimize conflicts.

+ **Provide engaging and relevant lessons:** Design lessons that are interesting, challenging, and relevant to students' lives. Engaged students are less likely to engage in disruptive behaviors and conflicts.

+ **Build strong teacher-student relationships:** Establish positive rapport with your students by actively listening to them, showing empathy, and being responsive to their needs. When students feel emotionally connected to their teacher, they are more likely to seek resolution instead of escalating conflicts.

Effective Communication Techniques

Communication plays a pivotal role in conflict resolution. Here are some effective communication techniques that teachers can utilize:

+ **Active listening:** Practice active listening by paying full attention to students' concerns, thoughts, and emotions. Validate their feelings and provide them with a safe space to express themselves.

+ **Nonviolent communication:** Teach students the principles of nonviolent communication, which emphasize empathy, understanding, and finding win-win solutions. Encourage students to express their needs and feelings in a respectful manner.

+ **Maintain a calm and respectful demeanor:** Model appropriate behavior during conflicts. Stay calm, composed, and respectful, even in difficult situations. Avoid using a confrontational or aggressive tone, as it can escalate conflicts further.

+ **Encourage dialogue and mediation:** Provide opportunities for students to engage in open discussions and problem-solving. Teach conflict resolution strategies such as compromise, negotiation, and seeking common ground. When conflicts arise, act as a mediator to guide students towards resolution.

Fostering a Supportive Classroom Culture

Creating a supportive classroom culture is foundational to conflict prevention and management. Here are some strategies to foster such an environment:

+ **Promote empathy and respect:** Teach students to value and respect diverse perspectives and backgrounds. Encourage them to empathize with their peers and develop a sense of understanding and acceptance.

+ **Implement restorative practices:** Introduce restorative practices, such as circles or conferences, where students can discuss their actions, make amends, and restore relationships. These practices help in resolving conflicts and building a sense of community.

+ **Encourage problem-solving skills:** Teach students problem-solving techniques, such as identifying the cause of conflicts, brainstorming solutions, and evaluating their effectiveness. By empowering students to find their own resolutions, they become active participants in conflict management.

+ **Promote reflection and self-awareness:** Encourage students to reflect on their behavior and its impact on themselves and others. Help them develop self-awareness and emotional intelligence, which are essential for conflict resolution and personal growth.

Challenges and Solutions

While proactive measures and effective communication techniques can help prevent and manage conflicts, challenges may still arise. Here are some common challenges teachers face and appropriate solutions:

+ **Power struggles:** Address power struggles by providing students with choices and opportunities for autonomy within established boundaries. Empower students through shared decision-making and student-centered approaches.

+ **Bullying and harassment:** Create a zero-tolerance policy for bullying and harassment. Implement clear consequences for such behaviors and provide support to both victims and perpetrators. Educate students about the importance of empathy and respect to combat bullying.

+ **Cultural misunderstandings:** Foster cultural sensitivity and understanding among students. Promote dialogue, appreciation, and curiosity about different cultures and perspectives. Address cultural conflicts through open-mindedness and education.

+ **Parental involvement:** Communicate openly with parents and involve them in conflict resolution processes when necessary. Seek their input and support in addressing conflicts that impact the student's learning environment.

Conclusion

Preventing and managing conflicts in the classroom requires proactive measures, effective communication techniques, and a supportive classroom culture. By promoting a positive environment, teaching conflict resolution skills, and addressing challenges, teachers can create a harmonious learning space where conflicts are minimized, and students thrive. Remember, conflict resolution is not only about resolving the immediate issue but also about teaching students lifelong skills in navigating disagreements and building positive relationships.

Section 2: Differentiated Instruction

Subsection 1: Understanding the principles of differentiated instruction

In this section, we will explore the principles of differentiated instruction, a teaching approach that recognizes and accommodates the diverse needs, interests, and learning styles of students. Differentiated instruction aims to promote inclusive learning environments where all students can thrive and reach their full potential.

Background

Education is not one-size-fits-all. Students come from varied backgrounds, possess different abilities, and have their own unique learning preferences. Traditional instructional methods may not effectively engage and support every student in the classroom. This is where differentiated instruction comes in.

Differentiated instruction is rooted in the belief that students learn best when instruction is tailored to their individual needs. It recognizes that students vary in their readiness, interests, and learning profiles, and thus requires teachers to adapt their instructional approaches to meet these diverse needs.

Principles of Differentiated Instruction

Differentiated instruction is guided by several key principles:

1. **Flexibility:** Differentiated instruction emphasizes flexibility in teaching. Teachers must be willing to modify and adapt their instructional methods and materials to accommodate the diverse needs of their students. This may involve providing varied resources, grouping students differently, or adjusting the pace of instruction.

2. **Individualization:** Differentiated instruction considers each student as an individual and seeks to provide personalized learning experiences. It involves understanding each student's strengths, weaknesses, interests, and learning preferences, and tailoring instruction accordingly. By acknowledging and valuing the unique qualities of each student, differentiated instruction fosters a positive and inclusive classroom culture.

3. **Assessment of Learning:** Differentiated instruction requires ongoing assessment to gather information about students' progress and understanding. This assessment helps teachers identify individual needs and determine appropriate instructional strategies. It also allows for timely feedback to students, enabling them to monitor their own learning and make necessary adjustments.

4. **Collaboration:** Differentiated instruction values collaboration and teamwork among teachers, students, and sometimes even parents or community members. By involving multiple perspectives and expertise, it enhances the learning experience and promotes a supportive learning community. Collaboration can take various forms, such as peer interaction, cooperative learning activities, or partnerships with external organizations.

5. **Inclusive Environment:** Differentiated instruction aims to create an inclusive environment where all students feel valued and supported. Teachers foster an atmosphere of respect, promote equity, and embrace diversity. By acknowledging and celebrating the unique contributions of each student, differentiated instruction creates a safe and nurturing learning space for all.

Practical Strategies

Implementing differentiated instruction requires a range of practical strategies. Here are some effective approaches:

1. **Tiered Assignments:** Tiered assignments offer different levels of complexity and challenge to students based on their readiness and skill level. This allows students to work at their own pace and ensures that all students are appropriately challenged.

2. **Learning Stations:** Learning stations provide different activities or materials at various stations within the classroom. Students rotate through these stations, engaging in activities that cater to their different interests and learning preferences. This strategy promotes active learning, independent thinking, and student choice.

3. **Flexible Grouping:** Flexible grouping involves organizing students into small groups based on their learning needs and interests. Groups can be formed based on ability level, learning style, or shared interests. Teachers can then tailor instruction to each group's specific needs and provide targeted support.

4. **Varied Assessments:** Differentiated instruction also involves providing varied assessments to evaluate student understanding and progress. This can include traditional tests, projects, presentations, or portfolios. By offering multiple assessment options, students can demonstrate their learning in ways that suit their strengths and preferences.

5. **Alternative Materials:** Differentiated instruction requires offering alternative materials to support different learning profiles. This can involve providing audio recordings, visual aids, manipulatives, or technology-based resources. By diversifying the materials, teachers accommodate different learning styles and enhance student engagement.

Examples and Resources

To better understand the principles and strategies of differentiated instruction, let's consider a real-world example. In an elementary school classroom, a teacher has a diverse group of students with varying abilities and interests. To differentiate an upcoming math lesson on fractions, the teacher creates three tiered assignments:

1. For students who have a solid understanding of fractions, they are assigned to work on complex word problems that require critical thinking and application of fraction concepts.

2. For students who require additional support, they are given manipulatives to visually represent fractions and practice basic fraction operations with hands-on activities.

3. For students who are ready to extend their learning, they are tasked with exploring equivalent fractions and comparing fractions using visual models and interactive technology tools.

This example illustrates how differentiation can be applied to meet the needs of different learners within the same classroom.

If you are interested in further exploring the principles and practices of differentiated instruction, the following resources may be helpful:

+ *Differentiated Instruction: A Guide for Middle and High School Teachers* by Amy Benjamin

+ *How to Differentiate Instruction in Academically Diverse Classrooms* by Carol Ann Tomlinson

+ *The Differentiated Classroom: Responding to the Needs of All Learners* by Carol Ann Tomlinson

+ *Teaching Gifted Kids in Today's Classroom: Strategies and Techniques Every Teacher Can Use* by Susan Winebrenner and Dina Brulles

Caveats and Challenges

Although differentiated instruction offers numerous benefits, it also presents challenges that educators need to address:

- Time Constraints: Designing and implementing differentiated instruction requires careful planning and preparation. Teachers must allocate sufficient time to develop differentiated materials, create flexible learning environments, and provide individualized support. Time management becomes crucial to ensure that all students receive the attention they need.

- Differentiating for Every Student: While it is ideal to differentiate instruction for every student, practical constraints may make it challenging to meet each student's unique learning needs all the time. Teachers must strike a balance between individualization and broader instructional goals to ensure effective learning for all students.

- Assessment and Feedback: Assessing and providing feedback for individual students in a differentiated classroom can be demanding. Teachers must develop efficient assessment strategies and provide timely, meaningful feedback to guide students' ongoing learning and growth. Utilizing various assessment methods can help address this challenge.

By acknowledging these challenges and seeking appropriate solutions, educators can maximize the benefits of differentiated instruction in their classrooms.

Conclusion

Differentiated instruction recognizes the diverse needs and capabilities of students and aims to create inclusive and engaging learning environments. By understanding the principles of differentiated instruction and implementing practical strategies, teachers can effectively address students' individual needs and promote their overall academic growth. With the right mindset, collaboration, and ongoing professional development, differentiated instruction has the potential to transform teaching and learning for the better.

Remember, differentiation is not about creating more work for teachers, but rather about meeting learners where they are and providing meaningful and relevant learning experiences. Embracing differentiated instruction can lead to increased student engagement, motivation, and academic success.

Now that we have explored the principles of differentiated instruction, let's continue our journey in the next section by examining strategies for designing and delivering differentiated lessons.

Subsection 2: Strategies for designing and delivering differentiated lessons

In this subsection, we will explore various strategies for designing and delivering differentiated lessons. Differentiated instruction is an approach that recognizes the diverse learning needs, abilities, and interests of students, and aims to provide them with personalized learning experiences. By tailoring instruction to meet individual needs, differentiated lessons can enhance student engagement, promote deeper understanding, and improve overall learning outcomes.

Understanding the principles of differentiated instruction

Before diving into the strategies, it is important to understand the principles that underpin differentiated instruction. These principles guide the design and delivery of lessons that accommodate the various learning profiles of students. Here are three key principles:

1. **Flexible Grouping:** Differentiation involves grouping students based on their needs, abilities, and learning styles. These groups can be fluid, and students may move between groups based on their progress or changing needs. Flexible grouping allows teachers to provide targeted instruction and support to individual students or small groups.

2. **Varied Instructional Strategies:** Differentiated instruction utilizes a range of teaching strategies to cater to diverse learning preferences. Teachers may employ direct instruction, collaborative learning, independent study, hands-on activities, or other instructional methods to engage students and address their unique needs.

3. **Assessment for Learning:** Assessment is an integral part of differentiated instruction. Teachers use ongoing formative assessment to gauge student progress, identify strengths and areas for growth, and make informed decisions about instructional adaptations. This allows teachers to provide timely feedback and adjust the learning experience to better suit each student.

By keeping these principles in mind, teachers can create a classroom environment that supports differentiated instruction.

Strategies for designing differentiated lessons

Designing differentiated lessons involves careful planning and consideration of the diverse needs of students. Here are some strategies that can help teachers create effective differentiated lessons:

1. **Pre-assessment:** Begin by assessing students' prior knowledge or skill levels before introducing new content. This can be done through informal discussions,

quick quizzes, or diagnostic assessments. Pre-assessment helps teachers identify students who may require additional support or those who are ready for more challenging tasks.

2. **Tiered Assignments:** Tiered assignments offer different levels of complexity within a single lesson, allowing students to work at their appropriate level. Teachers can modify the content, process, or product of an assignment to meet different students' needs. For example, in a history lesson, students could choose to write an essay, create a visual timeline, or produce a multimedia presentation based on their interests and abilities.

3. **Learning Contracts:** Learning contracts are agreements between teachers and students that outline the learning goals, activities, and assessment criteria for a given unit or project. Students have some choice in how they demonstrate their learning, and teachers provide guidance and support. Learning contracts promote self-directed learning and allow students to work at their own pace and interests.

4. **Station Rotation:** Station rotation involves dividing the classroom into different activity stations, each offering a different learning experience. Students rotate between stations, engaging in various tasks that address different learning styles or abilities. For example, one station could focus on hands-on experiments, while another could involve online research.

5. **Flexible Learning Pathways:** In this approach, teachers provide multiple pathways for students to achieve the learning goals. This may involve offering a selection of learning resources, allowing students to choose the order of tasks, or providing alternative assessments. By giving students autonomy and agency in their learning, flexible learning pathways promote engagement and motivation.

Delivering differentiated lessons

Once the lessons are designed, teachers need to effectively deliver differentiated instruction to meet the diverse needs of their students. Here are some strategies for delivering differentiated lessons:

1. **Small Group Instruction:** During whole-group instruction, teachers can form small groups to provide targeted instruction and support. This allows teachers to address specific needs, provide personalized feedback, and monitor progress. Small group instruction can be done during independent work time or through guided practice activities.

2. **Learning Stations:** As mentioned earlier, learning stations provide opportunities for students to engage in various activities. Teachers can facilitate and support students as they work at different stations, offering guidance,

answering questions, and providing feedback. This allows teachers to address individual needs while maintaining an active and engaging classroom environment.

3. **Individual Conferences:** Regular one-on-one conferences with students can provide valuable feedback and guidance. These conferences can be used to discuss individual goals, review progress, and provide additional support or extensions. Individual conferences also allow students to reflect on their learning and set new goals.

4. **Collaborative Learning Opportunities:** By encouraging students to work collaboratively, teachers can create opportunities for peer learning and support. Collaborative activities can involve problem-solving tasks, group projects, or discussions. In heterogeneous groups, students can learn from each other's strengths and receive guidance from peers.

5. **Technology Integration:** Technology can be a powerful tool for delivering differentiated instruction. It allows for personalized learning experiences, adaptive assessments, and access to a wide range of resources and learning materials. By leveraging educational technology, teachers can provide individualized support, track progress, and offer interactive and engaging learning experiences.

It is important to note that delivering differentiated lessons requires careful monitoring, adjustment, and reflection. Teachers should regularly assess student progress, gather feedback, and reflect on the effectiveness of their instructional strategies. By continuously refining their practice, teachers can ensure that differentiated instruction effectively meets the diverse needs of their students.

Example and resources

To illustrate the strategies for designing and delivering differentiated lessons, let's consider an example in a high school English class. The teacher wants to address different reading levels and interests while teaching a novel.

First, the teacher administers a pre-assessment to gauge students' reading comprehension levels. Based on the results, the teacher groups students into different reading level groups for small group instruction.

The teacher then designs tiered assignments that correspond to the different reading levels. Students can choose from various activities, such as creating a character analysis, writing a critical review, or participating in a book club discussion. The teacher provides resources and guidance to each group based on their needs and abilities.

During the lesson, the teacher implements learning stations, where students rotate between activities, such as reading excerpts from the novel, analyzing literary devices, or engaging in collaborative discussions. The teacher circulates among the stations, providing support, feedback, and addressing individual needs.

Throughout the unit, the teacher schedules individual conferences with students to discuss their progress, provide feedback, and set goals for improvement. The teacher also encourages peer collaboration by assigning group projects where students can work together to analyze themes or create multimedia presentations.

The teacher leverages technology by providing access to e-books, online discussion forums, and interactive quizzes. Students can engage with digital resources at their own pace and receive instant feedback on their progress.

To further support their practice, teachers can explore the following resources: - "Differentiated Instruction: A Guide for Middle and High School Teachers" by Amy Benjamin. - "The Differentiated Classroom: Responding to the Needs of All Learners" by Carol Ann Tomlinson. - The website Edutopia (https://www.edutopia.org/) offers various articles, videos, and case studies on differentiated instruction. - The ASCD (Association for Supervision and Curriculum Development) website (http://www.ascd.org/) provides resources, publications, and professional development opportunities related to differentiated instruction.

By implementing these strategies and utilizing available resources, teachers can successfully design and deliver differentiated lessons that cater to the diverse needs of their students.

Caveats and considerations

While differentiated instruction offers numerous benefits, there are some caveats and considerations to keep in mind:

1. **Time management:** Designing and delivering differentiated lessons requires careful planning and organization. It is crucial for teachers to allocate sufficient time for preparation, monitoring, and assessing student progress.

2. **Classroom management:** With the implementation of varied instructional strategies and flexible grouping, effective classroom management becomes vital. Teachers must establish clear expectations, routines, and procedures to ensure a productive and inclusive learning environment.

3. **Individualization versus differentiation:** While differentiation focuses on addressing students' diverse needs, it is essential to strike a balance between meeting individual needs and promoting cohesive classroom experiences. Teachers should find a middle ground where students receive tailored instruction without feeling isolated or excluded.

4. **Support and resources:** Implementing differentiated instruction may require additional support, such as professional development opportunities, collaboration with colleagues, or access to appropriate resources. Teachers should seek out these resources and establish a support network to enhance their practice.

By considering these caveats and continuously reflecting on their practice, teachers can navigate the complexities of differentiated instruction and provide meaningful learning experiences for all students.

Conclusion

Designing and delivering differentiated lessons is a crucial aspect of effective teaching. By understanding the principles of differentiated instruction and implementing strategies aligned with these principles, teachers can create personalized learning experiences that cater to diverse student needs. Through pre-assessment, tiered assignments, flexible learning pathways, and the use of various instructional approaches, teachers can engage and support students in their learning journey. By leveraging technology, collaborative learning opportunities, and individual conferences, teachers can further enhance differentiated instruction. With careful planning, reflection, and ongoing professional growth, teachers can make a positive impact on the learning outcomes of all students in their classrooms.

Subsection 3: Successful implementation of differentiated instruction in various subjects

Differentiated instruction is an approach to teaching and learning that recognizes the diverse needs, interests, and abilities of students. It involves adapting the content, process, and products of instruction to ensure student engagement and success. In this subsection, we will explore successful implementation strategies of differentiated instruction in various subjects.

Understanding differentiated instruction

Before delving into the implementation strategies, let's first understand the key principles of differentiated instruction. At its core, differentiated instruction aims to provide multiple pathways for students to acquire knowledge, make meaning, and demonstrate their learning. It acknowledges that students vary in their readiness to learn, interests, learning preferences, and strengths. By recognizing and responding to these differences, educators can create meaningful learning experiences for all students.

Identifying student needs and interests

To successfully implement differentiated instruction, teachers need to gather information about their students' needs, interests, and learning profiles. This can be done through formative assessments, observations, conversations, and student self-reflections. By understanding the unique characteristics of their students, teachers can tailor instruction to meet individual needs.

For example, in a science class, a teacher might discover that some students struggle with visualizing abstract concepts, while others excel in hands-on experiments. With this knowledge, the teacher can provide different resources, such as visual aids or hands-on activities, to support the diverse learning needs of their students.

Flexible grouping strategies

One of the key strategies in differentiated instruction is flexible grouping. It involves intentionally organizing students into different groups based on their instructional needs and interests. Flexible grouping can take various forms, such as whole-class instruction, small-group activities, or individualized learning.

In mathematics, for instance, a teacher may group students based on their proficiency level in a specific concept. Students who have a solid understanding of the concept can work collaboratively on challenging problems, while those who need additional support can receive personalized instruction from the teacher. This approach allows each student to work at their own pace and receive the necessary support or extension activities.

Tiered assignments

Another effective strategy in differentiated instruction is tiered assignments. Tiered assignments offer different levels of complexity and challenge, allowing students to access the content at their appropriate level. This approach ensures that all students are appropriately challenged and engaged in their learning.

For example, in a language arts class, a teacher may provide different reading assignments based on each student's reading level. Students who are proficient readers might be given more complex texts, while struggling readers receive texts at their instructional level. By providing tiered assignments, teachers can scaffold learning and ensure that all students are working at their own level of proficiency.

Choice boards or menus

Choice boards or menus provide students with a range of options for demonstrating their understanding of a topic or concept. These menus are designed to cater to students' varied interests, learning styles, and strengths. Students can choose from a menu of activities and assignments that align with their preferences and demonstrate their learning in a way that best suits them.

For instance, in a social studies class, a choice menu might include activities such as creating a timeline, writing a persuasive essay, or designing a multimedia presentation. By providing choices, students have the opportunity to showcase their learning in a way that resonates with their individual strengths and interests.

Technology integration

Technology can play a crucial role in implementing differentiated instruction. It offers a wide array of tools and resources that can support individualized learning and engage students in meaningful ways. Teachers can leverage technology to provide differentiated instruction through adaptive learning platforms, online resources, interactive simulations, and multimedia presentations.

For example, in a foreign language class, students can use language learning apps or websites to practice vocabulary and grammar skills at their own pace. These digital resources can provide instant feedback, personalized recommendations, and individualized pathways for students to improve their language proficiency.

Monitoring and adjusting instruction

Differentiated instruction requires ongoing monitoring of student progress and adjustment of instruction based on student needs. Formative assessments, such as quizzes, exit tickets, and observations, can help teachers gather feedback on student understanding and inform instructional decisions.

Teachers should regularly review student work, provide timely feedback, and make necessary adjustments to instruction. This continuous assessment and adjustment process ensures that the differentiated instruction is meeting the needs of all students and promotes their ongoing growth and achievement.

Real-world examples

To further illustrate the successful implementation of differentiated instruction, let's consider a real-world example in a physical education class. In this class, the teacher recognizes that students have different levels of fitness and interest in various physical activities. To address this, the teacher creates flexible grouping strategies by allowing students to choose from a variety of activities, such as running, yoga, or team sports. Students who are more advanced in their fitness level can engage in challenging workouts, while those who are beginners can focus on building their foundational skills. By differentiating instruction in this way, the teacher ensures that all students are actively engaged and learning at their own pace.

Caveats and challenges

While differentiated instruction offers many benefits, it also presents challenges that educators must navigate. Some challenges include the time required for planning and implementing differentiated lessons, managing diverse classroom dynamics, and ensuring equity and fairness in assessment. Teachers need ongoing professional development and support to effectively implement differentiated instruction and address these challenges.

Resources and further reading

For educators interested in exploring differentiated instruction further, here are some recommended resources:

- "Differentiation in Practice: A Resource Guide for Differentiating Curriculum" by Carol Ann Tomlinson
- "How to Differentiate Instruction in Mixed-Ability Classrooms" by Carol Ann Tomlinson
- "The Differentiated Classroom: Responding to the Needs of All Learners" by Carol Ann Tomlinson
- "Teaching Gifted Kids in Today's Classroom: Strategies and Techniques Every Teacher Can Use" by Susan Winebrenner

These resources provide practical strategies, examples, and case studies to support teachers in implementing differentiated instruction effectively.

Conclusion

Successful implementation of differentiated instruction in various subjects requires understanding student needs and interests, flexible grouping strategies, tiered assignments, choice boards or menus, technology integration, monitoring and adjusting instruction, and addressing challenges along the way. By employing these strategies, educators can create inclusive and engaging learning environments that promote student success. Differentiated instruction is a powerful approach that empowers students to reach their full potential and prepares them for a diverse and ever-changing world.

Subsection 4: Assessing and Adapting Instruction for Diverse Learners

Assessing the progress and learning outcomes of diverse learners is a critical aspect of effective teaching. In this subsection, we will explore different assessment strategies and techniques that can be employed to ensure equitable and inclusive instruction for all students.

Understanding Diverse Learners

Before discussing assessment strategies, it is important to develop an understanding of diverse learners. Diverse learners encompass students with varying cultural backgrounds, disabilities, learning styles, and abilities. As educators, it is crucial to recognize and respond to the unique characteristics and needs of each student.

To create an inclusive learning environment, teachers can gather information about their students through pre-assessment methods such as interviews, surveys, and observation. This initial information will help identify students' strengths, preferences, and areas in which they may need additional support. It is essential to remember that learners' abilities and needs may change over time, necessitating ongoing assessments and adaptations.

Formative Assessment

Formative assessment involves gathering real-time data on students' learning progress and using this information to modify teaching strategies and interventions. Here are some approaches to formative assessment specifically tailored to diverse learners:

- **Observation and Anecdotal Notes:** Regular observation of students during classroom activities provides valuable insights into their learning progress and engagement. Teachers can take anecdotal notes to record observations of individual students, noting their strengths, challenges, and areas for improvement. These observations can guide instructional decisions and help shape personalized learning plans.

+ **Questioning Techniques:** Effective questioning strategies allow teachers to assess students' understanding and misconceptions. Encouraging all students to participate by using techniques like think-pair-share or polling can provide a comprehensive picture of their learning. Open-ended questions can also reveal diverse perspectives and promote critical thinking among students with varied backgrounds and experiences.

+ **Self-assessment and Peer Assessment:** Involving students in assessing their own learning and providing feedback to their peers fosters metacognition and collaboration. Teachers can guide students to set goals, reflect on their progress, and evaluate their work based on predetermined criteria. Peer assessment can provide alternative perspectives and promote a supportive learning community.

Summative Assessment

While formative assessment focuses on providing ongoing feedback and shaping instruction, summative assessment is used to evaluate student achievement at the end of a unit, course, or academic year. When designing summative assessments for diverse learners, consider the following principles:

+ **Universal Design for Learning (UDL):** UDL principles ensure access and engagement for all learners. Provide multiple means of representation, expression, and engagement. For instance, offering assessment options in various formats (e.g., written, oral, visual) allows students to showcase their knowledge and skills using their preferred mode of communication.

+ **Scaffolding and Accommodations:** Accommodations and scaffolding support learners with diverse needs during summative assessments. Consider providing additional time, alternative formats, or assistive technologies to ensure equitable access. Differentiated instructions and accommodations should align with students' individualized education plans (IEPs) or 504 plans, promoting fairness and reducing barriers.

Data Analysis and Adaptation

Analyzing assessment data enables teachers to identify patterns, make data-informed decisions, and adapt instruction accordingly. Here are some steps to effectively analyze data and adapt instruction for diverse learners:

- **Identifying Trends:** Analyze assessment data at the class and individual levels to identify trends, such as common misconceptions, gaps in knowledge, or learning needs. Pay special attention to identify patterns related to diverse learners, ensuring their specific needs are addressed.

- **Grouping and Differentiation:** Use assessment data to group students with similar needs for targeted instruction. Differentiate instruction by providing supplementary materials, modified assignments, or enrichment activities based on students' assessed proficiency levels. Flexibility and adaptability are key when tailoring instruction to meet the needs of diverse learners.

- **Feedback and Goal Setting:** Use assessment data to provide meaningful feedback to students and guide their goal-setting process. Feedback should be specific, actionable, and personalized, addressing strengths and areas for growth. Encourage students to reflect on their progress, set goals, and create action plans to further their learning.

Case Study: Assessing Language Proficiency in a Diverse Classroom

Let's consider a case study involving a diverse classroom where students have varying levels of language proficiency. To assess and adapt instruction for these learners, the following steps can be taken:

1. Pre-Assessment: Administer a language proficiency survey to gather information about students' language background, experiences, and self-perceived abilities.

2. Formative Assessment: Use a combination of observation, questioning techniques, and project-based tasks to consistently monitor students' language development. Provide feedback on their speaking, reading, listening, and writing skills.

3. Summative Assessment: Design a performance-based task that assesses students' language proficiency, allowing them to demonstrate their abilities in a contextually rich and culturally responsive manner. Offer multiple assessment options, such as written or oral presentations, to accommodate diverse preferences and abilities.

4. Data Analysis and Adaptation: Analyze the assessment results to identify students' strengths, areas for improvement, and common language challenges. Group students based on their language proficiency levels and tailor instruction to meet their unique needs. Provide additional support, resources, or scaffolding to help students progress in their language development.

By using a combination of formative and summative assessment strategies and adapting instruction based on the data collected, educators can ensure equitable learning opportunities for diverse learners.

Resources for Assessing Diverse Learners

To further explore assessment approaches for diverse learners, the following resources can be helpful:

- **CAST:** The Center for Applied Special Technology (CAST) provides resources and tools for implementing Universal Design for Learning (UDL) principles in assessment. Their website offers practical guidelines, case studies, and strategies for creating inclusive assessments (https://www.cast.org/).

- **National Center on Universal Design for Learning:** The National Center on Universal Design for Learning offers resources for designing assessments that meet the needs of diverse learners. Their website provides examples, guidelines, and best practices for implementing UDL in assessments (http://www.udlcenter.org/).

- **The Understanding by Design Guide to Creating High-Quality Units:** This book by Grant Wiggins and Jay McTighe offers guidance on designing assessments aligned with desired learning outcomes. It provides insights into authentic assessment design and strategies for addressing diverse student needs.

Incorporating a range of assessment techniques that are sensitive to the needs of diverse learners supports inclusive and equitable instruction. By assessing and adapting instruction, educators can create a supportive learning environment where every student has the opportunity to thrive and succeed.

Subsection 5: Overcoming Challenges and Ensuring Equity in Differentiated Instruction

Differentiated instruction is an effective approach to accommodate the diverse learning needs of students in the classroom. However, it also presents various challenges that teachers must overcome to ensure equity and effectiveness. In this section, we will explore some common challenges faced in implementing differentiated instruction and provide strategies to address them.

Challenge 1: Time Constraints

One of the primary challenges in differentiated instruction is the allocation of sufficient time to plan, prepare, and implement various instructional strategies tailored to individual student needs. Teachers often struggle to find the time to create multiple lesson plans, design differentiated activities, and provide timely feedback. Moreover, managing multiple groups or individual tasks during classroom instruction may require additional time and effort.

To overcome this challenge, teachers can adopt the following strategies:

1. **Effective time management:** Prioritize essential concepts and skills, focus on core instructional goals, and allocate time accordingly. Streamline lesson planning by utilizing technology tools and resources that provide pre-designed differentiated activities.

2. **Collaboration and resource sharing:** Collaborate with colleagues and share resources to lighten the workload. Engage in professional learning communities or online platforms to exchange ideas, strategies, and resources for differentiated instruction.

3. **Gradual implementation:** Start with small differentiations and gradually expand to meet the needs of all students. This approach allows teachers to become comfortable with differentiated instruction over time, minimizing the initial time constraints.

Challenge 2: Classroom Management

Differentiated instruction often requires flexible grouping and adapting instructional strategies to meet the diverse needs of students. Managing multiple student groups or individual tasks simultaneously can be challenging, leading to disruptions, distractions, and unequal participation. Maintaining a positive and inclusive classroom environment is crucial for ensuring equity and engagement.

Here are some strategies to address this challenge:

1. **Clear expectations and routines:** Establish clear expectations for behavior, group work, and transitions. Teach students the necessary skills to work independently and collaboratively, ensuring smooth transitions between differentiated activities.

2. **Flexible and responsive instruction:** Anticipate potential challenges and have alternative strategies ready to address unexpected disruptions. Monitor individual student progress and provide timely interventions or support as needed.

3. **Student participation structures:** Implement structures such as think-pair-share, gallery walks, or jigsaw activities that encourage active participation and collaboration among students. Rotate group roles regularly to ensure equal opportunities for leadership and contribution.

Challenge 3: Assessment and Grading

Assessing and grading students' performance in a differentiated classroom can be complex, as students may be working on different tasks or mastery levels. Ensuring fair and accurate assessment practices is essential to maintain equity and provide meaningful feedback to students.

Consider the following strategies to address this challenge:

1. **Clear assessment criteria:** Communicate clear expectations and criteria to students for each differentiated task. Use rubrics or checklists that align with the learning objectives to guide assessment and provide feedback.

2. **Varied assessment methods:** Incorporate a variety of assessment methods, such as performance tasks, portfolios, self-reflections, or conferences, that allow students to demonstrate their learning in different ways. Ensure that assessment methods are accessible and appropriate for diverse learners.

3. **Formative assessment:** Regularly assess student progress during the learning process to identify individual needs and adjust instruction accordingly. Provide ongoing feedback that supports growth and guides students towards improvement.

Challenge 4: Equity and Access

Ensuring equity in differentiated instruction is essential to provide equal opportunities for all students to succeed. The challenge lies in addressing the diverse learning needs while avoiding tracking or creating hierarchies among students based on perceived abilities.

To promote equity and access, consider the following strategies:

1. **Universal Design for Learning (UDL):** Implement UDL principles to design instruction that is accessible and inclusive for all learners. Provide multiple means of representation, expression, and engagement to accommodate diverse learning styles and abilities.

2. **Differentiation based on strengths:** Differentiate instruction based on individual strengths and interests rather than perceived weaknesses. Offer opportunities for students to showcase their strengths and talents, fostering a positive and empowering learning environment.

3. **Flexible grouping:** Implement a variety of grouping strategies, including whole-group, small-group, and individual work, to ensure all students have the opportunity to collaborate and learn with diverse peers.

Challenge 5: Professional Development and Support

Implementing differentiated instruction effectively requires ongoing professional development and support for teachers. Many educators may lack the necessary training or resources to implement differentiated instruction successfully.

Consider the following strategies to address this challenge:

1. **Professional development opportunities:** Offer regular professional development sessions focused on differentiated instruction. Provide teachers with the knowledge, strategies, and resources needed to implement differentiated instruction effectively.

2. **Coaching and mentorship:** Pair teachers with experienced mentors or coaches who can provide guidance, feedback, and support in implementing differentiated instruction. Foster a collaborative culture where teachers can share successes, challenges, and seek advice from their colleagues.

3. **Access to resources:** Provide teachers with access to high-quality resources, including lesson plans, instructional materials, and technology tools, that

support differentiated instruction. Establish collaboration platforms or resource-sharing networks to facilitate access to resources and ideas.

Overcoming the challenges of implementing differentiated instruction requires a proactive and supportive approach. By addressing time constraints, classroom management, assessment and grading, equity and access, and providing ongoing professional development and support, teachers can create an inclusive and effective learning environment for all students.

Remember, differentiated instruction is a continuous journey, and each challenge presents an opportunity for growth and improvement. By embracing these challenges and implementing effective strategies, teachers can ensure equity and maximize the potential of differentiated instruction in the classroom.

Section 3: Technology Integration

Subsection 1: Benefits and Challenges of Technology Integration in Education

In today's digital age, technology plays a significant role in shaping modern education. The integration of technology in classrooms has the potential to enhance teaching and learning experiences, foster collaboration, and improve student engagement. However, along with its numerous benefits, there are also challenges that educators must navigate in order to effectively integrate technology into the educational environment. This subsection explores the benefits and challenges of technology integration in education, providing insights, examples, and strategies for successful implementation.

Benefits of Technology Integration

Technology integration in education offers a wide range of benefits for both teachers and students. Some of the key advantages include:

1. **Enhanced Learning Opportunities**: Technology provides students with access to a vast array of resources, including online databases, educational websites, and multimedia content. This wealth of information allows students to explore topics in greater depth and engage in self-directed learning.

2. **Improved Engagement and Motivation**: Integrating technology in the classroom can capture students' attention and make learning more exciting and interactive. Multimedia presentations, educational games, and virtual simulations can motivate students to actively participate in their learning journey.

3. **Personalized Instruction:** Technology enables teachers to tailor instruction to meet the individual needs and learning styles of students. Adaptive learning software and online platforms offer personalized learning pathways, allowing students to progress at their own pace and receive immediate feedback.

4. **Enhanced Collaboration:** Technology facilitates collaboration and communication among students and teachers. Online discussion forums, collaborative documents, and video conferencing tools enable students to work together on projects, share ideas, and receive feedback from their peers and educators.

5. **Development of 21st-century Skills:** Integrating technology in education fosters the development of essential skills for the 21st century, such as digital literacy, critical thinking, problem-solving, and creativity. These skills are crucial for success in the digital age and the future workforce.

Challenges of Technology Integration

While technology integration offers numerous benefits, it also presents some challenges that educators need to address. Understanding and effectively addressing these challenges will contribute to successful implementation. Some of the common challenges include:

1. **Access and Equity:** Ensuring equitable access to technology tools and internet connectivity is a significant challenge, particularly in economically disadvantaged areas. Schools must provide equal access to technology resources to bridge the digital divide and prevent further disparities in education.

2. **Infrastructure and Technical Support:** Implementing technology in classrooms requires a robust and reliable infrastructure, including internet connectivity, hardware, and software. School administrations need to invest in updating and maintaining the necessary infrastructure and providing adequate technical support.

3. **Teacher Training and Professional Development:** Integrating technology effectively requires teachers to have the necessary digital skills and technical knowledge. Providing ongoing professional development opportunities and training sessions will enable teachers to confidently integrate technology into their teaching practices.

4. **Digital Literacy and Responsible Use:** Technology integration necessitates developing students' digital literacy skills, including critical evaluation of online information and responsible use of digital tools. Educators must educate students about digital citizenship, online safety, and ethical use of technology.

5.   **Time and Curriculum Constraints:**   Integrating technology into the curriculum can create time constraints, as teachers need to plan and adapt their lessons to incorporate technology effectively.   It is crucial to strike a balance between technology integration and the existing curriculum goals and requirements.

Strategies for Successful Technology Integration

Addressing the challenges and successfully integrating technology into education requires careful planning and implementation.   Here are some strategies to facilitate successful technology integration:

1.   **Develop a Technology Integration Plan:**   Schools should develop a comprehensive technology integration plan that aligns with the educational goals and provides a roadmap for implementation.   The plan should include clear objectives, professional development opportunities, and strategies for addressing access and equity issues.

2. **Provide Ongoing Training and Support:** Teachers should receive ongoing training and professional development opportunities focused on integrating technology effectively.   This training should cover both technical aspects and instructional strategies to support effective technology integration.

3. **Focus on Pedagogy:** Technology should serve as a tool to enhance instruction and student learning outcomes, rather than a standalone solution. Teachers should consider how technology can support their instructional goals and engage students in active learning experiences.

4. **Promote Collaboration and Sharing:** Creating a culture of collaboration among educators can promote the sharing of best practices and strategies for effective technology integration.   Encouraging teachers to share their successes, challenges, and resources can lead to a collective improvement in technology integration practices.

5. **Address Equity and Access:** Schools should ensure equitable access to technology tools and resources for all students. This may include providing devices and internet connectivity to economically disadvantaged students or establishing technology resource centers within communities.

6. **Evaluate and Reflect:** Regular evaluation and reflection on technology integration initiatives are essential to assess their effectiveness.   Schools should establish mechanisms for collecting feedback from teachers, students, and parents to identify areas of improvement and make necessary adjustments.

By leveraging the benefits of technology integration while effectively addressing the associated challenges, educators can create innovative and engaging learning environments that prepare students for success in the digital age.

Real-World Example

A real-world example of successful technology integration can be seen in the "One Laptop per Child" (OLPC) initiative. This global project aims to provide every child with a rugged, low-cost, low-power laptop that is connected to the internet. The OLPC laptops are designed to enhance education and provide access to digital resources in developing countries.

Through the OLPC program, students have access to educational resources, online collaboration tools, and multimedia content. The laptops enable personalized learning experiences, promote student engagement, and foster the development of digital literacy skills.

The program faced various challenges, including infrastructure limitations and providing support and training to teachers. However, through strategic partnerships, ongoing monitoring and evaluation, and continuous improvement, the OLPC initiative has made significant progress in integrating technology into education and improving learning outcomes for children in underserved communities.

Conclusion

Technology integration in education offers numerous benefits, including enhanced learning opportunities, improved engagement, and personalized instruction. However, challenges such as access and equity issues, infrastructure limitations, and the need for teacher training must be effectively addressed to ensure successful implementation.

By developing comprehensive technology integration plans, providing ongoing training and support, focusing on pedagogy, promoting collaboration, and addressing equity and access, educators can overcome challenges and create meaningful learning experiences that prepare students for the future. Real-world initiatives, like the OLPC program, demonstrate the potential of technology integration to bridge educational gaps and empower learners worldwide.

Subsection 2: Strategies for integrating technology effectively into teaching and learning

In today's digital age, technology has become an integral part of our lives, including education. Integrating technology effectively into teaching and learning can enhance engagement, collaboration, and creativity among students. However, to maximize the benefits of technology, educators need to employ strategies that align with educational goals and pedagogical principles. In this subsection, we will explore a range of strategies for integrating technology in the classroom.

Strategy 1: Define clear learning objectives

Before incorporating technology into classroom activities, it is essential to clearly define the learning objectives. Technology should be used as a tool to facilitate and enhance student learning, rather than as a mere flashy gadget. By identifying the desired learning outcomes, teachers can select appropriate technological tools and activities that align with the curriculum. For example, if the objective is to improve students' research skills, choosing online databases, virtual libraries, or search engines can be beneficial.

Strategy 2: Select appropriate technological tools

The market is flooded with various educational technologies, making it crucial for educators to carefully select tools that cater to their specific instructional needs. Consider factors such as ease of use, compatibility with existing technology infrastructure, student accessibility, and cost-effectiveness. For instance, interactive whiteboards, educational apps, and digital simulations are popular tools that can engage students and enhance their understanding of complex concepts.

Strategy 3: Provide professional development and support

To effectively integrate technology, teachers need to possess the necessary knowledge and skills themselves. Professional development programs and ongoing support can equip educators with the competencies required to integrate technology effectively into their teaching practices. Schools can organize workshops, training sessions, or online courses to enhance teachers' digital literacy and empower them to make informed decisions about technology integration.

Strategy 4: Foster collaborative learning through technology

Technology can facilitate collaborative learning by enabling students to work together on projects, share ideas, and provide feedback. Tools such as online discussion forums, collaborative documents, and video conferencing platforms can create opportunities for students to collaborate both inside and outside the classroom. For example, teachers can use online platforms to assign group projects, where students can collaborate virtually and contribute to a shared document or presentation.

Strategy 5: Embrace a blended learning approach

Blended learning combines traditional face-to-face instruction with online learning activities. By incorporating online components such as virtual lectures, online quizzes, or discussion boards, teachers can personalize learning experiences, promote self-directed learning, and cater to different learning styles. Blended learning can also free up classroom time for interactive activities, discussions, and hands-on experiences.

Strategy 6: Assess and provide feedback using technology

Technology offers various ways to assess student learning and provide timely feedback. Online quizzes, interactive assessments, and electronic portfolios can provide immediate feedback to students, allowing them to monitor their progress and identify areas for improvement. Teachers can also use learning management systems or education software to track student performance, generate reports, and provide targeted feedback.

Strategy 7: Consider accessibility and equity

When integrating technology into teaching and learning, it is crucial to ensure that all students have equal access and opportunities. Consider students with disabilities, limited internet access, or those who may not possess personal devices. Implement strategies such as providing alternative formats, offering technology resources in the classroom, or organizing computer lab sessions to bridge the digital divide and ensure equitable access to learning opportunities.

Strategy 8: Stay updated on emerging technologies

Technology is constantly evolving, and new educational tools and resources are continuously being developed. It is essential for educators to stay updated on emerging technologies and explore their educational potential. Professional networks, online communities, and education conferences can provide opportunities to learn about innovative technologies, discuss best practices, and discover new ways to integrate technology effectively into teaching and learning.

In conclusion, integrating technology effectively into teaching and learning requires careful planning, ongoing professional development, and alignment with learning goals. By applying strategies such as defining clear learning objectives, selecting appropriate technological tools, fostering collaboration, embracing blended learning, and considering accessibility, educators can create engaging and meaningful learning experiences that leverage the power of technology. Remember, technology is only a tool; it is the skillful integration and thoughtful pedagogy that make it transformative in the educational landscape.

Subsection 3: Examples of successful technology integration initiatives

In this subsection, we will explore various examples of successful technology integration initiatives in education. These examples demonstrate how technology can be effectively used to enhance teaching and learning experiences, promote engagement and collaboration, and support students' acquisition of knowledge and skills.

Example 1: Flipped Classroom Model in a High School Science Class

In a high school science classroom, the teacher implemented the flipped classroom model to create an interactive and student-centered learning environment. The teacher used online videos and resources to deliver lecture content outside the classroom, allowing students to watch and review the material at their own pace. During class time, students engaged in hands-on activities, experiments, and discussions to apply what they learned from the pre-class videos.

The use of technology in this flipped classroom approach provided students with flexibility in accessing and reviewing the content. It also allowed the teacher to dedicate more class time to practical applications and deeper discussions. Students reported increased engagement and a deeper understanding of the subject matter as a result of this technology-based approach.

Example 2: Collaborative Online Projects in a Language Arts Class

In a middle school language arts class, the teacher integrated technology by engaging students in collaborative online projects. Students were assigned to small groups and used online platforms to collaborate on writing stories, creating newsletters, or researching and presenting on specific topics. By leveraging technology, students were able to work together in real-time, regardless of their physical location.

This technology integration initiative promoted student collaboration, critical thinking, and communication skills. It also provided students with an authentic audience for their work, as they could easily share their projects with classmates, parents, and even a wider online community. The use of technology in this setting expanded opportunities for creativity and enhanced students' digital literacy skills.

Example 3: Virtual Reality Field Trips in a Social Studies Class

In a middle school social studies class, the teacher utilized virtual reality (VR) technology to take students on virtual field trips. Through VR headsets, students were transported to historical periods, archaeological sites, and geographical locations relevant to their curriculum. They could explore ancient civilizations, experience historical events, and immerse themselves in cultural landmarks, enhancing their understanding of the subject matter.

The integration of VR technology in social studies provided students with immersive and engaging learning experiences. It allowed them to visualize and interact with historical and geographical contexts, making abstract concepts more tangible and memorable. This technology-based approach sparked students' curiosity, stimulated discussions, and fostered a deeper appreciation for the topics studied.

Example 4: Adaptive Learning Software in a Math Class

In an elementary school math class, the teacher incorporated adaptive learning software to cater to the diverse needs of students. The software provided personalized practice exercises and adaptive feedback based on individual student performance and learning styles. It offered additional support and challenges as needed, ensuring that each student progressed at their own pace.

The integration of adaptive learning software in this math class promoted individualized instruction, allowing students to work at their own level and receive immediate feedback. It also provided the teacher with valuable data on students' progress and areas for intervention. Students showed improvement in their math skills and developed a sense of ownership over their learning.

These examples highlight the potential of technology integration in education. By leveraging technology effectively, educators can create innovative and engaging learning environments that cater to diverse learners' needs. However, it is important to note that successful technology integration requires careful planning, ongoing support, and proper training for teachers. Additionally, the selection of appropriate technological tools should align with curricular goals and pedagogical approaches.

Subsection 4: Evaluating the impact of technology on student achievement

The integration of technology in education has brought about significant changes in teaching and learning practices. However, it is crucial to evaluate the impact of technology on student achievement to ensure its effectiveness and identify areas for improvement. In this subsection, we will discuss various methods and approaches for evaluating the impact of technology on student achievement.

Quantitative Measures

Quantitative measures provide numerical data to assess the impact of technology on student achievement. These measures allow for statistical analysis and comparison between different groups or conditions. Here are some commonly used quantitative measures:

1. **Standardized Test Scores:** Standardized tests are widely used to measure student achievement across different subjects and grade levels. By comparing the test scores of students who have access to technology with those who do not, we can examine the impact of technology on academic performance.

2. **GPA (Grade Point Average):** GPA is a quantitative measure of a student's overall academic performance. It can be used to assess the impact of technology on student achievement by comparing the GPAs of students who use technology regularly with those who do not.

3. **Attendance and Dropout Rates:** Technology can enhance student engagement and motivation, which may lead to improved attendance and reduced dropout rates. By analyzing attendance and dropout data of students in technology-enhanced classrooms, we can evaluate the impact of technology on student achievement.

4. **Time-on-Task:** Technology can provide opportunities for more active and interactive learning experiences. Measuring the time students spend actively engaged with technology tools and resources can help evaluate the impact of technology on their achievement.

Quantitative measures provide valuable insights into the impact of technology on student achievement. However, it is important to consider other factors that might influence student outcomes, such as student characteristics, instruction quality, and school environment.

Qualitative Measures

Qualitative measures provide in-depth insights into the impact of technology on student achievement. They involve gathering rich, descriptive data through interviews, observations, and open-ended surveys. Here are some commonly used qualitative measures:

1. **Interviews:** Conducting interviews with students, teachers, and parents can help gather perceptions and experiences regarding the impact of technology on student achievement. Open-ended questions can elicit detailed responses, allowing for a deeper understanding of the complexities involved.

2. **Observations:** Observing students using technology in the classroom provides a firsthand account of the impact on their learning experiences. This can include observing student engagement, collaboration, problem-solving, and critical thinking skills.

3. **Student Portfolios:** Student portfolios showcase their work and progress over time. By examining the quality and depth of students' work using technology, we can assess the impact on their achievement in terms of creativity, critical thinking, and the application of knowledge.

4. **Teacher Reflections:** Teachers can provide insights into the impact of technology on student achievement through reflective practices. They can analyze their instructional strategies, student outcomes, and changes in teaching practices resulting from the integration of technology.

Qualitative measures provide valuable insights into the impact of technology on student achievement by capturing the nuanced experiences and perceptions of students and teachers. These measures can help identify the factors that contribute to the success or challenges associated with technology integration.

Mixed-Methods Approach

A mixed-methods approach combines both quantitative and qualitative measures to provide a holistic understanding of the impact of technology on student achievement. By integrating multiple types of data, researchers can triangulate their findings and gain a more comprehensive view of the topic.

For example, a study evaluating the impact of a specific educational app on student achievement might collect quantitative data through pre- and post-tests to measure the improvement in test scores. Additionally, researchers may conduct interviews or focus groups to gather qualitative data on student experiences and perceptions.

The mixed-methods approach allows researchers to gain a deeper understanding of the complex relationship between technology and student achievement. It provides a more comprehensive picture by integrating different types of data and perspectives.

Caveats and Considerations

When evaluating the impact of technology on student achievement, it is essential to consider several caveats and factors that may influence the results. Here are some key considerations:

+ **Contextual Factors:** The impact of technology on student achievement can vary depending on the specific educational context, such as grade level, subject area, and socio-economic factors. These contextual factors should be taken into account when interpreting the results.

+ **Sustainability:** Evaluating short-term impacts might not provide a complete understanding of the long-term effects of technology on student achievement. Longitudinal studies are needed to assess the sustainability of the impact over time.

+ **Equity and Access:** Technology should not exacerbate existing achievement gaps. It is essential to consider issues of equity and access when evaluating the impact of technology on student achievement and ensure that all students have equal opportunities to benefit from technology integration.

+ **Teacher Professional Development:** The impact of technology on student achievement is significantly influenced by the capacity and readiness of teachers to effectively integrate technology into their instruction. Providing adequate professional development and support for teachers is crucial for maximizing the impact of technology on student achievement.

Overall, evaluating the impact of technology on student achievement requires a comprehensive approach that considers both quantitative and qualitative measures, as well as the contextual factors and caveats discussed above. By employing rigorous evaluation methods, researchers and educators can make informed decisions about the integration of technology and its potential impact on student learning outcomes.

Subsection 5: Future trends and emerging technologies in education

As education continues to evolve and adapt to the changing needs of learners and society, it is important to examine the future trends and emerging technologies that have the potential to shape the field. In this section, we will explore some of the exciting developments in education and how they can enhance teaching and learning experiences.

Virtual Reality (VR) and Augmented Reality (AR) in Education

Virtual Reality (VR) and Augmented Reality (AR) technologies have gained significant attention in recent years, and their potential in education is immense. These technologies offer immersive and interactive experiences that can enhance learning and engagement.

In virtual reality, students can be transported to different environments and engage in realistic simulations. For example, history students can virtually visit ancient civilizations or biology students can explore the human body. This hands-on approach can deepen understanding and make learning more memorable.

Augmented reality, on the other hand, layers digital information onto the real world, enhancing the physical environment with a digital overlay. AR can be used to provide additional information or interactive elements in textbooks, posters, or museum exhibits. This technology can transform traditional learning materials into interactive and engaging resources.

Both VR and AR can inspire creativity and critical thinking, allowing students to become active participants in their learning. As these technologies continue to advance and become more accessible, we can expect to see them integrated into various subjects and disciplines, creating new and exciting learning opportunities.

Artificial Intelligence (AI) in Education

Artificial Intelligence (AI) has revolutionized many industries, and education is no exception. AI has the potential to personalize learning experiences, provide real-time feedback, and support educators in various ways.

One of the key applications of AI in education is adaptive learning systems. These systems use machine learning algorithms to analyze student data and tailor instruction to individual needs. Adaptive learning platforms can identify students' strengths and weaknesses, provide personalized recommendations, and track progress over time. This level of personalization can help students learn at their own pace and address their specific learning needs.

AI can also automate administrative tasks, freeing up time for teachers to focus on instruction and building meaningful relationships with students. For example, chatbots powered by AI technology can answer common student queries and provide guidance outside of regular class hours. This can improve accessibility and support for learners, ensuring that they have the information they need when they need it.

Additionally, AI can assist in assessing student work. Automated grading systems can analyze essays, quizzes, and other assignments, providing instant feedback to students. While this technology is not meant to replace human grading entirely, it can help educators save time and provide timely feedback to students, allowing for more efficient and effective learning experiences.

Gamification and Game-Based Learning

Gamification and game-based learning have gained popularity in recent years, offering innovative approaches to engage and motivate learners. By applying game design elements and principles to educational contexts, educators can create immersive and interactive learning experiences.

Gamification involves adding game-like elements, such as points, badges, and leaderboards, to non-game activities. These elements can increase motivation, foster healthy competition, and reward students for their achievements. For example, a language learning app can award points and badges to learners who complete lessons or reach certain milestones. These incentives can create a sense of achievement and encourage learners to continue their progress.

Game-based learning, on the other hand, integrates educational content into games. This approach allows students to learn through active participation, problem-solving, and decision-making within the game. For instance, a physics game can present challenges that require players to apply scientific principles to advance in the game. By connecting learning objectives with game mechanics, students can develop critical thinking skills and enhance their understanding of the subject matter.

Through gamification and game-based learning, educators can tap into the inherent motivation and engagement that games provide. By making learning fun and interactive, these approaches can foster a positive learning environment and increase students' interest and participation.

Blockchain Technology in Education

Blockchain technology, often associated with cryptocurrencies like Bitcoin, has the potential to transform various industries, including education. Blockchain is a decentralized and distributed ledger that records transactions in a secure and transparent manner.

In education, blockchain technology can be used for credentialing and record-keeping. Currently, verifying academic credentials can be time-consuming and often requires contacting multiple institutions. With blockchain, educational records can be securely stored and easily verified by employers, institutions, or other stakeholders. This can streamline the hiring process and provide a more reliable and efficient way of verifying educational qualifications.

Furthermore, blockchain technology can enable the development of lifelong learning portfolios and micro-credentials. Learners can collect digital badges or certificates for completing specific courses or acquiring new skills. These credentials can be stored on the blockchain, allowing individuals to build a comprehensive record of their learning and accomplishments. Employers can then verify these credentials, gaining a more detailed understanding of an individual's skills and competencies.

While blockchain technology is still in its early stages of implementation in education, its potential for secure record-keeping and credentialing is promising. As the technology continues to mature, we can expect to see more widespread adoption and integration into educational systems.

Ethical Considerations and Challenges

While the future trends and emerging technologies present exciting possibilities for education, it is important to consider the ethical implications and challenges they may pose.

Data privacy and security are critical concerns when adopting these technologies. Educators and policymakers must ensure that student data is handled responsibly and protected from potential breaches. Clear protocols and guidelines need to be established to address these concerns and protect the rights of learners.

Furthermore, the digital divide remains a significant challenge that needs to be addressed. Access to technology and reliable internet connectivity can vary across different regions and communities. To ensure equitable access to these emerging technologies, efforts should be made to bridge the digital divide and provide equal opportunities for all learners.

Lastly, it is essential to strike a balance between technology and human interactions. While these emerging technologies can enhance teaching and learning experiences, they should not replace the valuable role of educators. Teachers play a crucial role in guiding and supporting students, fostering social interactions, and facilitating meaningful discussions. Technology should be seen as a tool to augment and enhance these interactions, rather than replace them.

Overall, the future trends and emerging technologies highlighted in this section have the potential to revolutionize education. By embracing these technologies, educators can create engaging and personalized learning experiences that promote student success and prepare learners for the challenges of the future.

Chapter 3: The Role of Research in Shaping Modern Education

Section 1: Evidence-Based Practice in Education

Subsection 1: Introduction to evidence-based practice and its importance in education

In recent years, evidence-based practice has emerged as a powerful approach to inform decision-making in various fields, including education. This subsection provides an introduction to evidence-based practice and highlights its importance in shaping effective teaching and learning strategies. We will explore the key principles of evidence-based practice, discuss its role in promoting student achievement, and examine the benefits it offers to educators.

Background

Evidence-based practice (EBP) is a systematic process that involves integrating the best available research evidence with professional expertise and considering the unique context and characteristics of learners to make informed decisions. While the concept of evidence-based practice originated in the field of medicine, it has gained significant recognition and application in education.

The goal of evidence-based practice in education is to bridge the gap between research and practice, ensuring that teaching and learning strategies are grounded in sound empirical evidence. By adopting an evidence-based approach, educators can enhance their effectiveness in the classroom and improve student outcomes.

Principles of Evidence-Based Practice

To effectively apply evidence-based practice in education, it is important to understand its key principles. These principles provide a foundation for using research evidence to inform decision-making and improve educational practices.

1. Systematic Approach: Evidence-based practice involves a systematic and structured process of identifying, critically appraising, and synthesizing relevant research evidence. This ensures that decisions are based on high-quality research and not influenced by personal biases or opinions.

2. Integration of Research Evidence: Educators must integrate research evidence with their professional expertise and knowledge of students' needs and backgrounds. It is essential to consider the characteristics of learners, the learning environment, and other contextual factors when applying research findings to practice.

3. Assessment of Research Quality: Assessing the quality and validity of research studies is crucial in evidence-based practice. Educators need to critically evaluate research methodologies, sample sizes, validity of measures, and other factors that may impact the reliability of the evidence.

4. Continuous Learning and Reflection: Evidence-based practice requires ongoing learning and reflection. Educators should regularly update their knowledge and skills based on the latest research findings and evaluate the effectiveness of their instructional practices.

The Role of Evidence-Based Practice in Education

The importance of evidence-based practice in education cannot be overstated. It offers valuable insights and guidance for educators to make informed decisions about instructional strategies, classroom management techniques, and other aspects of teaching and learning. Here are some key reasons why evidence-based practice is essential in education:

1. Improving Student Achievement: Evidence-based practice helps identify effective instructional strategies and interventions that have been shown to improve student achievement. By implementing evidence-based practices, educators can enhance learning outcomes and foster academic success for all students.

2. Enhancing Teaching Effectiveness: Evidence-based practice equips educators with the tools and knowledge to enhance their teaching effectiveness. By incorporating evidence-based instructional strategies, teachers can maximize student engagement, promote critical thinking, and meet the diverse learning needs of their students.

3.   Promoting Data-Driven Decision Making: Evidence-based practice encourages educators to use data and research evidence to guide decision-making. By analyzing student data and considering research findings, educators can tailor their instructional practices to address specific learning needs, leading to more effective teaching.

4. Enhancing Professional Development: Evidence-based practice promotes ongoing professional learning and development.   Educators can engage in evidence-based discussions, attend professional development workshops, and collaborate with colleagues to stay updated with the latest research findings and best practices.

5.   Building Trust and Accountability: Evidence-based practice establishes transparency and accountability in education.   It helps build trust among stakeholders, including students, parents, administrators, and policymakers, who can have confidence in the effectiveness of educational practices backed by robust research evidence.

Examples of Evidence-Based Practice in Education

To illustrate the practical application of evidence-based practice in education, let's consider two examples:

1. Phonics Instruction: Research has consistently shown that explicit phonics instruction, which teaches the relationship between letters and sounds, is highly effective in improving reading skills. Educators who adopt evidence-based phonics instruction methods can help students develop strong reading foundations and improve overall literacy outcomes.

2.   Cooperative Learning: Evidence-based practice supports the use of cooperative learning strategies, which involve students working together in small groups to achieve shared learning goals.   Research suggests that cooperative learning promotes social interaction, active engagement, and higher levels of achievement among students.

Resources and Caveats

Implementing evidence-based practice in education requires access to reliable sources of research evidence and resources. Educators can leverage the following resources to support evidence-based decision-making:

1. Research Journals: Academic journals such as "Educational Researcher," "American Educational Research Journal," and "Review of Educational Research" publish rigorous studies and meta-analyses that inform evidence-based practices.

2. Research Clearinghouses: Online platforms like the What Works Clearinghouse (WWC) and the Campbell Collaboration provide educators with access to systematic reviews and evidence summaries on a wide range of educational interventions and strategies.

While evidence-based practice offers numerous benefits, it is essential to recognize the limitations and caveats associated with its implementation. Educators must consider the contextual factors, resources, and constraints of their specific educational setting when applying research findings to practice. Additionally, evidence-based practice should not replace professional judgment or individualized educational planning. It should be used as a complementary approach to inform decision-making and improve teaching and learning practices.

Exercises

1. Select a topic of interest in education (e.g., classroom management, reading instruction, math problem-solving). Using online research databases, locate three research articles that provide evidence-based practices related to your chosen topic. Summarize the findings and discuss how these practices can inform your teaching.

2. Discuss with your colleagues or fellow educators the challenges and opportunities of implementing evidence-based practice in your school or educational setting. Share examples of successful evidence-based interventions that have been implemented and reflect on their impact.

3. Analyze a current teaching practice that you use in your classroom. Explore research literature and examine the evidence supporting this practice. Based on the evidence, evaluate whether the practice aligns with evidence-based principles and consider potential modifications or alternatives.

Conclusion

Evidence-based practice is a powerful approach that enhances teaching and learning in education. By integrating research evidence with professional expertise and considering the unique needs of students, educators can make informed decisions that support student achievement and promote effective instructional practices. By engaging in evidence-based practice, educators contribute to an evidence-informed educational system that continuously evolves and improves to meet the needs of learners.

Subsection 2: Evaluating and using research evidence in decision-making

In the field of education, decision-making is a critical aspect of ensuring the success of educational practices. However, it is important to base these decisions on solid research evidence to ensure that they are effective and have a positive impact on teaching and learning outcomes. This subsection focuses on the process of evaluating and using research evidence in decision-making, providing teachers and educators with the necessary tools to make informed choices.

Importance of research evidence in decision-making

Decision-making in education should be guided by research evidence to ensure that the chosen strategies and interventions are backed by rigorous scientific findings. When educators rely on evidence-based practices, they can have confidence in the effectiveness of their decisions and improve the likelihood of positive outcomes for students. It also helps in avoiding ineffective or potentially harmful practices.

By evaluating research evidence, teachers and educators can make informed choices that are more likely to lead to improved student achievement, engagement, and well-being. Research evidence also provides a basis for justifying and explaining decisions to stakeholders such as parents, administrators, and policymakers.

Process of evaluating research evidence

Evaluating research evidence involves a systematic and critical analysis of relevant studies to determine their methodological rigor, validity, and applicability to the specific educational context. Here are the key steps involved in this process:

1. **Identify the research question:** Start by clearly defining the specific question or issue that needs to be addressed. This will help focus the search for relevant research evidence.

2. **Conduct a literature review:** Search for and gather relevant research studies and articles that address the identified research question. Use reputable sources such as peer-reviewed journals and academic databases.

3. **Assess the quality of the research studies:** Evaluate the methodological quality of the studies to determine their reliability and validity. Consider factors such as the study design, sample size, data collection methods, and statistical analysis.

4. **Consider the relevance and generalizability:** Assess whether the findings of the research studies are applicable to the specific educational context. Consider factors such as the population studied, the intervention or strategy used, and the outcomes measured.

5. **Evaluate the strength of the evidence:** Consider the consistency and magnitude of the effect sizes reported in the studies. Look for evidence of statistical significance and practical significance.

6. **Consider potential biases:** Be aware of potential biases in the research studies, such as publication bias or conflicts of interest. Assess the credibility and objectivity of the researchers and funding sources.

7. **Synthesize the evidence:** Analyze and interpret the findings of the research studies. Look for patterns, trends, and consistencies across multiple studies. Consider both the quantitative and qualitative evidence.

8. **Apply the findings to the educational context:** Once the research evidence has been evaluated, consider how it can be applied to the specific educational context. Identify the implications for teaching and learning practices and determine the feasibility of implementation.

Using research evidence in decision-making

Using research evidence in decision-making involves translating the findings into practical strategies and interventions that can be implemented in the classroom or educational setting. Here are some key considerations when using research evidence:

+ **Tailor the evidence to the context:** While research evidence provides valuable insights, it is important to consider the unique characteristics of the students, school, and community. Adapt the findings to fit the specific context and needs.

+ **Collaborate with stakeholders:** Involve key stakeholders, such as teachers, administrators, parents, and students, in the decision-making process. Seek their input, perspectives, and feedback to ensure the decisions align with their needs and expectations.

+ **Monitor and evaluate the impact:** Implementing evidence-based practices should be an ongoing process. Monitor the implementation and evaluate the impact of the strategies and interventions. Adjust and refine as needed based on feedback and data.

+ **Professional development and support:** Provide teachers and educators with the necessary professional development and support to implement evidence-based practices effectively. Offer training, resources, and ongoing coaching to build their capacity.

+ **Continued research and learning:** Education is an evolving field, and new research evidence continues to emerge. Stay updated with the latest research findings and engage in continuous learning to enhance your decision-making skills.

Example: Evaluating the effectiveness of a reading intervention

To illustrate the process of evaluating and using research evidence in decision-making, let's consider an example of evaluating the effectiveness of a reading intervention for struggling readers. The research question is: "Does a phonics-based reading intervention improve reading outcomes for struggling readers in elementary schools?"

1. **Identify the research question:** The research question is whether a phonics-based reading intervention improves reading outcomes for struggling readers.

2. **Conduct a literature review:** Search for and gather relevant research studies that evaluate the effectiveness of phonics-based reading interventions for struggling readers.

3. **Assess the quality of the research studies:** Evaluate the methodological quality of the studies by examining factors such as the study design, sample size, and measurement of reading outcomes.

4. **Consider the relevance and generalizability:** Assess whether the findings of the studies are applicable to the specific elementary school context and population of struggling readers.

5. **Evaluate the strength of the evidence:** Consider the consistency and magnitude of the effect sizes reported in the studies. Look for evidence of statistical significance and practical significance.

6. **Consider potential biases:** Examine any potential biases in the studies, such as publication bias or conflicts of interest. Assess the credibility and objectivity of the researchers and funding sources.

7. **Synthesize the evidence:** Analyze and interpret the findings of the studies. Look for patterns and consistencies across multiple studies to determine the overall effectiveness of phonics-based reading interventions for struggling readers.

8. **Apply the findings to the educational context:** Consider how the research evidence can be applied to the specific elementary school context. Determine the implications for teaching practices and assess the feasibility of implementing a phonics-based reading intervention.

Based on the evaluation of the research evidence, if multiple studies consistently demonstrate the positive impact of phonics-based reading interventions on reading outcomes for struggling readers, the decision to implement such an intervention in the elementary school would be supported. However, it is important to consider factors such as the availability of resources, teacher expertise, and support needed for effective implementation.

Resources for evaluating research evidence

Several resources and tools are available to help educators evaluate research evidence. Some examples include:

- The What Works Clearinghouse (WWC): The WWC is an online resource that provides educators with access to evidence-based education research. It reviews and rates the quality of research studies and provides summaries of effective educational programs and practices.

- The National Center for Education Evaluation and Regional Assistance (NCEE): The NCEE conducts rigorous evaluations of educational programs, practices, and policies. Their reports provide valuable insights into the effectiveness of various interventions and strategies.

- Journal of Educational Psychology, American Educational Research Journal, and other reputable peer-reviewed journals: These journals publish research articles that undergo a rigorous review process, ensuring the quality of the studies published.

- Professional learning communities and networks: Collaborating with colleagues and engaging in discussions with other educators can provide opportunities to share experiences and insights about research evidence in education.

Caveats and considerations

While research evidence is crucial for informed decision-making, it is essential to recognize its limitations and complexities. Here are some caveats and considerations to keep in mind:

+ Research evidence should be considered alongside professional expertise and contextual factors. It is not a one-size-fits-all solution but rather an informed guide for decision-making.

+ Not all research evidence is of equal quality. It is important to critically evaluate the methodological rigor and validity of the studies before drawing conclusions or making decisions based on their findings.

+ Context matters. Research evidence may not directly apply to every educational setting due to variations in student characteristics, school resources, and cultural factors. Adaptation and contextualization are essential.

+ Research evidence should be considered as part of a broader decision-making process that includes input from teachers, administrators, parents, and students. Collaborative decision-making ensures a more comprehensive and inclusive approach.

Conclusion

Evaluating and using research evidence in decision-making is a fundamental aspect of promoting effective educational practices. By critically evaluating the quality, relevance, and applicability of research studies, educators can make informed choices that have a positive impact on teaching and learning outcomes. By applying the findings of research evidence to the specific educational context and involving key stakeholders, educators can enhance the effectiveness and success of their practices.

Subsection 3: Case studies of evidence-based practices in different educational settings

In this subsection, we will explore several case studies that showcase the successful implementation of evidence-based practices in various educational settings. These case studies highlight the importance of using research evidence to inform decision-making and improve teaching and learning outcomes.

Case Study 1: Implementing a Growth Mindset Intervention

One evidence-based practice that has gained significant attention in recent years is the implementation of growth mindset interventions. A growth mindset refers to the belief that abilities and intelligence can be developed through dedication and hard work. This concept was popularized by psychologist Carol Dweck and has been shown to have a positive impact on student motivation, resilience, and academic achievement.

In a study conducted by Blackwell et al. (2007), a growth mindset intervention was implemented in a diverse middle school. The intervention involved teaching students about the malleability of intelligence and providing strategies to foster a growth mindset. Results showed that students who received the intervention demonstrated greater effort, higher grades, and an increase in the belief that intelligence can be developed. This study highlights the potential of growth mindset interventions in improving student outcomes.

Case Study 2: Peer Tutoring for Mathematics Education

Peer tutoring is another evidence-based practice that has shown promising results in improving student learning outcomes, particularly in mathematics education. Peer tutoring involves students working together in pairs or small groups, with one student serving as the tutor and the other as the tutee. This approach promotes active learning, collaboration, and the opportunity for students to explain concepts to one another.

A study conducted by Newman et al. (2013) explored the effectiveness of peer tutoring in a middle school mathematics classroom. Results showed that students who participated in peer tutoring sessions outperformed their peers who did not receive the tutoring. The tutoring sessions provided an opportunity for students to engage in deep learning, clarify misconceptions, and develop a deeper understanding of mathematical concepts. This case study highlights the benefits of peer tutoring as an evidence-based practice in promoting student learning in mathematics.

Case Study 3: Flipped Classroom Approach in Higher Education

The flipped classroom approach is an evidence-based practice that has gained popularity in higher education. In a flipped classroom, the traditional lecture-based content delivery is moved outside the class, typically through the use of pre-recorded videos or readings, while the in-class time is dedicated to active learning activities and discussions. This approach allows students to engage with course material outside of class and facilitates deeper learning during face-to-face sessions.

A study by Lage et al. (2000) examined the impact of the flipped classroom approach in a college-level engineering course. The researchers found that students in the flipped classroom group consistently outperformed those in the traditional lecture-based group. Students in the flipped classroom group reported higher levels of engagement, increased interaction with peers and instructors, and greater satisfaction with the learning experience. This case study demonstrates the effectiveness of the flipped classroom approach in promoting student engagement and learning outcomes in higher education.

Case Study 4: Mindfulness-Based Interventions for Student Well-being

Promoting student well-being is an important aspect of education. Mindfulness-based interventions have emerged as evidence-based practices that can enhance student well-being, reduce stress, and improve mental health outcomes. Mindfulness involves paying attention to the present moment without judgment, and it has been shown to have various positive effects on student academic and social-emotional outcomes.

A study by Zoogman et al. (2015) examined the impact of a mindfulness-based intervention on high school students. The intervention included mindfulness training sessions and activities designed to cultivate awareness and attention. Results showed that students who participated in the intervention reported reduced stress, increased self-compassion, and improved overall well-being. This case study highlights the potential of mindfulness-based interventions in promoting student well-being and mental health.

Overall, these case studies demonstrate the importance of evidence-based practices in education. By incorporating research findings into educational settings, educators can enhance teaching and learning outcomes, promote student well-being, and create a positive impact on student success. It is essential for educators to stay informed about the latest research in order to make evidence-informed decisions and practices in their classrooms.

Subsection 4: Challenges and potential solutions in implementing evidence-based practices

Implementing evidence-based practices in education can be a challenging task. Educators and policymakers often face various obstacles and barriers that hinder the adoption and effective implementation of evidence-based strategies. In this subsection, we will explore some of the common challenges and potential solutions to overcome them.

Challenges in implementing evidence-based practices

1. **Lack of awareness and knowledge:** Many educators, especially those who have limited access to professional development opportunities, may be unaware of the latest research and evidence-based practices in education. This lack of awareness can prevent them from implementing effective strategies in their classrooms.

2. **Resistance to change:** Resistance to change is a common challenge when introducing evidence-based practices in education. Teachers may feel comfortable with their existing teaching methods and may be reluctant to adopt new approaches that require a shift in their instructional practices.

3. **Time constraints:** Teachers often have limited time available for planning and implementing evidence-based practices. The pressure to cover the curriculum and meet assessment requirements can make it challenging to dedicate the necessary time for implementing new strategies.

4. **Limited resources and support:** Implementing evidence-based practices may require additional resources, such as technology tools, training materials, or specialized instructional strategies. Lack of funding and support from school administrators can hinder the successful implementation of these practices.

5. **Overemphasis on standardized testing:** In many educational systems, there is an overemphasis on standardized tests, which can lead to a narrow focus on test preparation rather than the implementation of evidence-based practices that promote deeper learning and critical thinking skills.

Potential solutions

1. **Professional development and training:** Providing educators with regular professional development opportunities can enhance their awareness and knowledge of evidence-based practices. Professional development should focus on translating research into practical strategies that can be implemented in the classroom.

2. **Early exposure and mentoring:** Introducing evidence-based practices early in teacher preparation programs and providing mentorship opportunities can help educators develop the necessary skills and confidence to implement these practices effectively.

3. **Flexible curriculum and scheduling:** School administrators can support the implementation of evidence-based practices by providing a flexible curriculum and

scheduling that allows teachers to have dedicated time for planning and collaboration.

4. **Resource allocation and support:** Allocating resources and providing support for implementing evidence-based practices is crucial. School administrators should provide teachers with the necessary tools, materials, and technology required to implement these practices successfully.

5. **Strategic assessment practices:** Rethinking assessment practices to align with evidence-based practices is essential. Moving away from solely relying on standardized tests and embracing formative assessments that provide timely and constructive feedback can encourage the adoption of evidence-based strategies.

6. **Creating a culture of collaboration and innovation:** Fostering a culture of collaboration and innovation within schools can support the implementation of evidence-based practices. Encouraging teachers to share successes and challenges, providing opportunities for peer observation and feedback, and celebrating innovative practices can promote the adoption of evidence-based strategies.

Overall, implementing evidence-based practices in education requires a systematic and thoughtful approach. Overcoming the challenges associated with the adoption of these practices requires a combination of awareness, support, resources, and a commitment to ongoing professional development. By addressing these challenges and implementing potential solutions, educators can improve student outcomes and create a more effective and engaging learning environment.

Subsection 5: Promoting a Culture of Evidence-Based Practice in Education

In the field of education, the adoption of evidence-based practices is crucial for improving teaching and learning outcomes. Evidence-based practice involves using the best available research evidence, combined with professional expertise and the needs and preferences of students, to inform educational decision-making and instructional practices. By promoting a culture of evidence-based practice, educators can ensure that their teaching methods are effective, efficient, and based on the latest research findings.

Background

The concept of evidence-based practice originated in the medical field, where it has been widely adopted to guide clinical decision-making and improve patient outcomes. In recent years, the application of evidence-based practice has extended to other disciplines, including education. By incorporating research evidence into educational practices, educators can make informed decisions about teaching strategies, curriculum design, assessment methods, and interventions.

Principles of Evidence-Based Practice in Education

Promoting a culture of evidence-based practice in education requires following a set of principles:

1. **Identifying the best available evidence:** Educators need to stay updated on the latest research findings in their field of expertise. This involves regularly reviewing peer-reviewed studies, meta-analyses, systematic reviews, and other high-quality sources of evidence. By critically evaluating research, educators can determine which practices are supported by evidence and align with their teaching context.

2. **Integrating research evidence with professional expertise:** While research evidence provides valuable insights, it is crucial to combine it with professional expertise. Educators have unique knowledge of their students, classroom dynamics, and school context. By integrating research evidence with their practical experience, educators can develop effective strategies that are tailored to their specific teaching environment.

3. **Considering student needs and preferences:** Evidence-based practice puts students at the center of decision-making. Educators need to consider the diverse needs, learning styles, and cultural backgrounds of their students when adapting research findings to their practice. By incorporating student input and individualizing instruction, educators can create a student-centered learning environment.

4. **Continuously evaluating and improving practice:** Evidence-based practice is an ongoing process of inquiry and reflection. Educators should regularly assess the effectiveness of their instructional methods and make adjustments based on evidence. This involves collecting data, analyzing outcomes, and reflecting on the impact of their teaching practices on student learning. By engaging in continuous improvement, educators can refine their instructional approaches and promote better learning outcomes.

Engaging in Evidence-Based Practice

Promoting a culture of evidence-based practice requires the active involvement of educators, administrators, and policymakers. Here are some strategies to foster an evidence-based culture in education:

- **Provide professional development:** Educators need training and support to develop the skills necessary for implementing evidence-based practices. Professional development workshops, seminars, and online courses can equip educators with the knowledge and tools to critically evaluate research evidence and incorporate it into their teaching practices.

- **Establish research-practice partnerships:** Collaboration between researchers and educators is essential for bridging the gap between research and practice. Research-practice partnerships involve ongoing collaboration, where researchers and educators work together to identify relevant research questions, conduct studies, and translate research findings into actionable strategies for the classroom. These partnerships facilitate the use of evidence in decision-making and ensure that research remains relevant and applicable to real-world educational settings.

- **Support a culture of inquiry:** Creating a culture of inquiry involves fostering curiosity, critical thinking, and a commitment to continuous improvement among educators. Schools and educational institutions can provide resources and platforms for educators to engage in collaborative inquiries, action research, and professional learning communities. By encouraging educators to critically examine their teaching methods and share insights with their peers, a culture of inquiry can be established.

- **Promote evidence dissemination and utilization:** It is important to create channels for sharing research evidence and best practices with educators, administrators, and policymakers. This can be done through conferences, publications, online platforms, and professional networks. Additionally, schools and districts can establish mechanisms for translating research findings into practical resources, such as instructional guides, toolkits, and databases, to facilitate the adoption of evidence-based practices.

- **Develop a supportive policy environment:** Policymakers play a crucial role in promoting evidence-based practice in education. They can create policies that incentivize the use of research evidence in decision-making, provide funding for research-practice partnerships, and support professional development initiatives. By aligning policies with evidence-based principles, policymakers can create an environment that values and supports evidence-based practice.

Challenges and Considerations

Promoting a culture of evidence-based practice in education comes with its own set of challenges and considerations:

+ **Access to research evidence**: Access to high-quality research evidence can be a challenge for educators, especially those working in resource-constrained settings. Efforts should be made to increase access to academic journals, research databases, and other sources of evidence. Open access initiatives, collaboration with research institutions, and the use of pre-print repositories can help overcome these challenges.

+ **Time and workload constraints**: Educators often face time and workload constraints that may limit their ability to engage in evidence-based practice. Schools and districts should provide educators with dedicated time and support to engage in professional development, research-practice partnerships, and collaborative inquiry. Integration of evidence-based practices into existing professional development programs and curriculum frameworks can also help address these constraints.

+ **Resistance to change**: Resistance to change and a preference for traditional practices can be a barrier to adopting evidence-based approaches. Creating a supportive and non-judgmental environment, promoting the benefits of evidence-based practice, and showcasing success stories can help overcome resistance and foster a culture of evidence-based practice.

+ **Ethical considerations**: Ethical considerations, such as informed consent, privacy, and data protection, need to be addressed when integrating research evidence into everyday practice. Educators and researchers should follow ethical guidelines and obtain necessary permissions when using student data for research purposes. Clear communication and collaboration between educators, researchers, and ethical review boards can help ensure that ethical considerations are addressed.

Conclusion

Promoting a culture of evidence-based practice is crucial for improving teaching and learning outcomes in education. By integrating research evidence with professional expertise and student needs, educators can make informed decisions and implement effective instructional strategies. By providing professional development, establishing research-practice partnerships, supporting a culture of inquiry, promoting evidence dissemination, and developing supportive policies, stakeholders in education can work together to create an environment that values and utilizes evidence-based practices. Overcoming challenges and addressing ethical considerations are important considerations in this process. By embracing evidence-based practice, educators can enhance their teaching effectiveness and ultimately improve student achievement and success.

Section 2: Educational Neuroscience

Subsection 1: Overview of educational neuroscience and its applications in teaching and learning

Educational neuroscience is an interdisciplinary field that combines neuroscience, psychology, and education to better understand how the brain learns and how this knowledge can inform teaching and learning practices. In this subsection, we will provide an overview of educational neuroscience and explore its applications in the classroom.

Background

The field of neuroscience has advanced rapidly in recent years, providing valuable insights into the inner workings of the brain. Educational neuroscience seeks to bridge the gap between neuroscience research and educational practice, translating scientific findings into practical strategies that can enhance teaching and learning outcomes.

Neurons and Brain Plasticity: The brain is composed of billions of specialized cells called neurons, which communicate with each other through electrochemical signals. When we learn something new, connections between neurons called synapses are strengthened, enabling the formation of new neural networks. This ability of the brain to reorganize and adapt is known as brain plasticity.

Cognitive Processes and Brain Regions: Different cognitive processes, such as attention, memory, and problem-solving, are associated with specific brain regions.

For example, the prefrontal cortex is involved in executive functions, such as decision-making and self-regulation, while the hippocampus plays a crucial role in memory formation. Understanding the relationship between cognitive processes and brain regions can help educators design effective instructional strategies.

Principles of Educational Neuroscience

Educational neuroscience is guided by several key principles that are essential for translating research findings into educational practices.

Interdisciplinarity: Educational neuroscience brings together expertise from different disciplines, including neuroscience, psychology, and education. This interdisciplinary approach allows researchers to consider multiple perspectives and develop comprehensive strategies for improving teaching and learning.

Individual Differences: The brain is unique to each learner, and educational neuroscience recognizes the importance of individual differences in learning. Understanding how different learners process information can inform the design of personalized learning experiences that cater to individual needs and strengths.

Developmental Perspective: The brain undergoes significant changes throughout development, and educational neuroscience takes into account the developmental stage of the learners when designing instructional strategies. It recognizes the importance of tailoring teaching methods to align with the cognitive abilities and learning preferences of the learners.

Evidence-Based Practice: Educational neuroscience emphasizes the use of evidence-based practices, rooted in scientific research, to guide teaching and learning. By critically evaluating research findings, educators can make informed decisions about instructional approaches that have been shown to be effective in enhancing learning outcomes.

Applications in Teaching and Learning

Educational neuroscience has numerous applications in the classroom, offering insights into how to optimize teaching and learning experiences. Here, we highlight some key areas of application.

Understanding Learning Processes: Educational neuroscience helps educators gain a deeper understanding of how learning occurs, enabling them to tailor instructional strategies to optimize learning outcomes. It provides insights into factors such as attention, memory, motivation, and metacognition, which are critical for effective learning.

Enhancing Memory Retention: Neuroscience research has identified strategies that enhance memory retention. For example, the use of spaced practice, interleaving different topics, and providing retrieval practice can improve long-term memory storage.

Promoting Engagement and Motivation: By understanding how the brain responds to different types of stimuli, educators can design engaging and motivating learning experiences. Incorporating elements such as novelty, relevance, and autonomy can activate the brain's reward system and enhance learner engagement.

Addressing Learning Difficulties: Educational neuroscience offers valuable insights into the underlying causes of learning difficulties. By identifying specific brain processes that are compromised in learners with learning disabilities, educators can develop targeted interventions to support their learning needs.

Optimizing Brain-Compatible Learning Environments: Classroom environments that align with how the brain learns best can enhance student engagement and learning outcomes. Factors such as lighting, temperature, and classroom arrangement can influence cognitive processes and attention.

Challenges and Ethical Considerations

While educational neuroscience holds immense promise for improving teaching and learning, it also presents challenges and ethical considerations that need to be carefully addressed.

Complexity and Limitations: The brain is an incredibly complex organ, and there is still much we do not know about how it functions. Educational neuroscience must navigate the limitations of current scientific knowledge, ensuring that recommendations are based on robust evidence rather than speculation.

Ethical Use of Neurotechnologies: The field of educational neuroscience involves the use of neuroimaging technologies, such as functional magnetic resonance imaging (fMRI), to study the brain. Ethical considerations regarding consent, privacy, and potential risks associated with these technologies need to be carefully addressed in research and educational settings.

Neuro-myths and Misinterpretation: The popularity of educational neuroscience has led to the proliferation of neuro-myths—misinterpretations or misapplications of neuroscience findings in educational contexts. Educators need to critically evaluate claims and ensure that evidence-based practices are implemented.

Resources and Further Reading

Educational neuroscience is a rapidly evolving field, and there are many resources available for educators interested in learning more. Some recommended readings include:

- *The Neuroscience of Learning and Development: Enhancing Creativity, Compassion, Critical Thinking, and Peace in Education* by Marilee Sprenger

- *Neuroteach: Brain Science and the Future of Education* by Glenn Whitman and Ian Kelleher

- *Mind, Brain, and Education Science: A Comprehensive Guide to the New Brain-Based Teaching* by Tracey Tokuhama-Espinosa

Additionally, organizations such as the International Mind, Brain, and Education Society (IMBES) and the Learning and the Brain Conference offer valuable resources and professional development opportunities for educators interested in educational neuroscience.

Conclusion

Educational neuroscience provides valuable insights into how the brain learns and how this knowledge can be applied to enhance teaching and learning practices. By understanding the principles of educational neuroscience and its applications in the classroom, educators can optimize instructional strategies, promote engagement and motivation, and address individual learning needs. It is an exciting field that has the potential to revolutionize education and improve learning outcomes for all learners.

Subsection 2: Understanding Brain Development and Its Implications for Education

The field of educational neuroscience investigates the relationship between brain development and learning, providing valuable insights for educators. Understanding how the brain develops can help educators optimize teaching strategies, curriculum design, and classroom environments to support effective learning. In this section, we will explore the principles of brain development and discuss their implications for education.

Principles of Brain Development

The human brain undergoes significant changes throughout childhood and adolescence, shaping cognitive abilities and learning capacities. Here are some key principles of brain development:

1. **Neuroplasticity:** The brain is highly plastic, meaning it can change and adapt in response to experiences. This property enables lifelong learning and the formation of new neural connections.

2. **Sensitive Periods:** Certain periods in development are particularly sensitive to specific types of learning. For example, language acquisition is most optimal during early childhood, while abstract reasoning skills develop during adolescence.

3. **Frontal Lobe Development:** The prefrontal cortex, which is responsible for executive functions such as decision-making, impulse control, and working memory, undergoes significant development during adolescence. This has implications for self-regulation and academic performance.

4. **Emotional Regulation:** Brain regions involved in emotional processing, such as the amygdala and the prefrontal cortex, develop in tandem. This development impacts emotional regulation and social-emotional learning.

5. **Synaptic Pruning:** During adolescence, there is a process of synaptic pruning, where unnecessary neural connections are eliminated. This refinement increases brain efficiency but also affects learning and memory consolidation.

Implications for Education

Understanding the principles of brain development can inform instructional practices and educational policies. Here are some implications for education:

1. **Creating Enriched Environments:** Providing stimulating and enriching learning environments can promote neuroplasticity and enhance brain development. This includes exposing students to a variety of experiences and offering opportunities for exploration and discovery.

2. **Taking Advantage of Sensitive Periods:** Recognizing the existence of sensitive periods in brain development, educators can design instruction that aligns with the developmental readiness of students. For example, early

language exposure and phonics instruction can optimize language acquisition.

3. **Supporting Executive Functions:** Considering the ongoing development of the prefrontal cortex, educators can implement strategies to support the development of executive functions. This includes providing scaffolding for decision-making, teaching self-regulation skills, and incorporating activities that promote working memory.

4. **Nurturing Emotional Intelligence:** Given the simultaneous development of emotion-related brain regions, promoting emotional intelligence can enhance students' emotional regulation and social skills. Educators can incorporate activities that foster empathy, self-awareness, and conflict resolution into the curriculum.

5. **Optimizing Learning and Memory:** Understanding synaptic pruning can inform instructional design. Educators can reinforce essential concepts and skills to ensure that neural connections are strengthened while being mindful of cognitive load to prevent overload.

Example: Math Education

Let's consider an example of how understanding brain development can influence math education. Research shows that the ability to solve complex mathematical problems relies on the development of the prefrontal cortex, which is still maturing in adolescence. To support students' mathematical abilities, educators can:

+ Provide opportunities for metacognitive reflection, which enhances executive functions involved in problem-solving.

+ Scaffold complex problem-solving tasks by breaking them down into smaller, manageable steps.

+ Allow for collaborative learning experiences, as social interactions can stimulate brain regions associated with mathematical reasoning.

+ Use visual representations and manipulatives to support spatial reasoning, which is linked to mathematical proficiency.

By aligning instructional strategies with the principles of brain development, educators can optimize learning experiences and support students in achieving their full potential in mathematics and other subject areas.

Resources and Further Reading

For further exploration of brain development and its implications for education, here are some valuable resources:

- Jensen, E. (2018). *Teaching with the Brain in Mind.* Association for Supervision and Curriculum Development.

- Willis, J., & Willis, D. (2007). *Research-Based Strategies to Ignite Student Learning: Insights from a Neurologist and Classroom Teacher.* Association for Supervision and Curriculum Development.

- Center on the Developing Child at Harvard University. (n.d.). *Brain Architecture.* Retrieved from `http://developingchild.harvard. edu/science/key-concepts/brain-architecture/`

These resources provide in-depth explanations and practical strategies for leveraging brain development in educational contexts.

Conclusion

Understanding brain development and its implications for education can revolutionize teaching practices and enhance learning outcomes. By embracing the principles of brain plasticity, sensitive periods, and frontal lobe development, educators can create supportive learning environments and design effective instructional strategies. By nurturing students' emotional intelligence and optimizing learning experiences, educators play a vital role in shaping the future of education.

Subsection 3: Neuroscience-informed Instructional Strategies

In recent years, the field of neuroscience has made significant strides in understanding how the brain functions and how we learn. This knowledge has great potential for informing and improving instructional strategies in education. In this subsection, we will explore some neuroscience-informed instructional strategies that can enhance teaching and learning outcomes.

Principles of Neuroscience in Education

Neuroscience in education is a multidisciplinary field that integrates findings from neuroscience, psychology, and education. It seeks to leverage our understanding of brain processes to inform teaching practices and create optimal learning environments. Here are some key principles that underpin neuroscience-informed instructional strategies:

1. **Engagement and Attention**: The brain is more likely to learn and retain information when learners are actively engaged and focused. Teachers can enhance engagement by incorporating elements such as hands-on activities, interactive discussions, and real-world examples.

2. **Emotion and Learning**: Emotions play a crucial role in learning and memory. Positive emotions, such as curiosity and interest, can enhance motivation and facilitate information processing. On the other hand, negative emotions, such as stress and fear, can impede learning. Creating a supportive and positive learning environment can help optimize learning outcomes.

3. **Memory and Retrieval**: Understanding how memory works can help teachers design effective instructional strategies. The brain engages in encoding, storage, and retrieval of information. Encouraging regular practice, promoting spaced repetition, and providing opportunities for retrieval practice can strengthen memory recall and retention.

4. **Multisensory Learning**: The brain processes information through multiple sensory modalities. Integrating visual, auditory, and kinesthetic elements in instruction can enhance learning outcomes. Incorporating visual aids, interactive demonstrations, and hands-on activities can stimulate different parts of the brain and promote deeper understanding.

5. **Individual Differences**: Every learner is unique, and understanding individual differences can inform instructional strategies. Variations in learning styles, cognitive abilities, and background knowledge should be considered when designing instruction. Personalized learning approaches that cater to individual needs can optimize learning experiences.

Neuroscience-informed Instructional Strategies

Based on the principles of neuroscience, educators can incorporate the following strategies to enhance teaching and learning outcomes:

1. **Active Learning**: Encourage students to actively participate in the learning process. This can be achieved through collaborative group work, hands-on

experiments, and problem-solving activities. Active learning promotes engagement, critical thinking, and knowledge application.

2. **Metacognition:** Metacognition refers to the awareness and control of one's own learning process. Teachers can teach students metacognitive strategies, such as self-reflection, goal setting, and self-assessment. These strategies help students become aware of their learning progress and make adjustments accordingly.

3. **Chunking and Spacing:** Breaking down complex information into smaller, manageable chunks can facilitate learning and retention. Additionally, spacing out learning sessions over time enhances long-term memory. Encourage students to review and revisit previously learned material periodically for better consolidation of knowledge.

4. **Incorporating Emotions:** Creating a positive and emotionally supportive classroom environment can enhance learning outcomes. Teachers can incorporate elements of surprise, humor, and storytelling to engage students emotionally. This emotional connection can improve motivation, attention, and memory.

5. **Multisensory Instruction:** Engaging multiple senses in instruction can enhance learning outcomes. Incorporate visual aids, auditory cues, and kinesthetic activities that appeal to different learning styles and modalities. This ensures that information is processed through multiple channels, leading to better understanding and retention.

6. **Feedback and Reflection:** Providing timely and constructive feedback helps students understand their progress and areas for improvement. Encourage students to reflect on their learning process and set goals for further growth. This promotes metacognition and self-regulated learning.

Example: Neuroscience-informed Math Instruction

Let's consider an example of applying neuroscience-informed instructional strategies in the context of math education. Traditional math instruction often focuses on rote memorization and procedural understanding. However, a neuroscience-informed approach would emphasize conceptual understanding and active engagement.

Incorporating the principles of neuroscience, math teachers can incorporate the following strategies:

1. **Hands-on Manipulatives:** Use concrete manipulatives, such as blocks or counters, to help students visualize mathematical concepts. This multisensory approach engages different parts of the brain and enhances understanding.

2. **Real-World Applications:** Connect math concepts to real-world contexts to make learning meaningful and relevant. For example, when teaching fractions, relate them to sharing food or dividing objects. This taps into students' prior knowledge and increases engagement.

3. **Collaborative Problem Solving:** Provide opportunities for students to work collaboratively on math problem-solving tasks. This promotes active learning, metacognition, and critical thinking skills. Students can discuss strategies, justify their reasoning, and learn from each other's perspectives.

4. **Frequent Retrieval Practice:** Incorporate regular retrieval practice to strengthen long-term memory. This can involve quizzes, quick problem-solving activities, or concept mapping exercises. Regular retrieval helps reinforce learning, identify gaps in knowledge, and enhance retention.

By applying neuroscience-informed instructional strategies, math teachers can create a more engaging and effective learning experience for their students, ultimately leading to improved understanding and achievement in math.

Caveats and Considerations

While neuroscience-informed instructional strategies offer valuable insights, it is important to acknowledge their limitations and be cautious in their implementation. Here are some caveats and considerations:

+ **Individual Differences:** Students have unique learning styles and preferences. It is essential to consider the diverse needs of learners and adapt instructional strategies accordingly.

+ **Ethical Considerations:** Neuroscience research should be conducted ethically, respecting the privacy and well-being of participants. It is crucial to obtain informed consent and ensure the ethical application of neuroscientific findings in educational settings.

+ **Collaboration with Neuroscientists:** Collaboration between educators and neuroscientists can further enhance the development and application of neuroscience-informed instructional strategies. This interdisciplinary approach ensures the integration of evidence-based practices and promotes ongoing research in education.

Further Resources

For educators interested in exploring neuroscience-informed instructional strategies further, the following resources may be helpful:

+ *Neuroteach: Brain Science and the Future of Education* by Glenn Whitman and Ian Kelleher

+ *Neuroscience and Education: A Comprehensive Guide* edited by Richard E. Mayer and Patricia A. Alexander

+ The Learning Scientists website (www.learningscientists.org) provides research-based resources and strategies for effective learning and teaching.

+ The National Institute for Learning Outcomes Assessment (www.learningoutcomesassessment.org) offers resources and tools for assessing student learning outcomes in higher education.

In conclusion, neuroscience-informed instructional strategies provide valuable insights into how the brain learns and can enhance teaching and learning outcomes. By incorporating active learning, metacognition, chunking, emotional engagement, multisensory instruction, and providing feedback, educators can optimize the learning experiences for their students. However, it is important to consider individual differences, ethical considerations, and collaborate with neuroscientists to ensure the responsible application of neuroscience findings in education.

Subsection 4: Ethical considerations and potential risks of educational neuroscience

Educational neuroscience is an emerging field that aims to leverage insights from neuroscience to inform educational practices and improve learning outcomes. While the potential benefits of educational neuroscience are significant, it is also important to critically examine the ethical considerations and potential risks associated with its implementation. This subsection will explore these issues in detail to provide a well-rounded understanding of the field.

Ethical Considerations in Educational Neuroscience

1. **Informed Consent:** One of the primary ethical considerations in educational neuroscience research is obtaining informed consent from participants. In educational settings, this can involve obtaining consent from both students and their parents. It is essential to ensure that participants fully understand the nature of the research, its potential implications, and any risks involved. Researchers should also provide clear information about the voluntary nature of participation and the right to withdraw at any time.

2. **Privacy and Confidentiality:** Educational neuroscience research often involves collecting sensitive information, such as brain imaging data or genetic samples, which could potentially reveal personal traits or conditions. It is crucial to protect the privacy and confidentiality of participants by anonymizing data and implementing secure storage and access protocols. Additionally, researchers should obtain consent for data sharing and clearly communicate any potential risks associated with the storage and use of participant data.

3. **Benefits versus Risks:** When conducting educational neuroscience research, it is essential to carefully consider the balance between the potential benefits and the potential risks to participants. Researchers should thoroughly evaluate the potential benefits of the research, such as the development of personalized instructional strategies or the identification of neurobiological markers for learning difficulties. However, researchers must also minimize any potential risks, such as physical discomfort during neuroimaging procedures or the potential stigmatization of students based on their neurological profiles.

4. **Equity and Fairness:** Educational neuroscience has the potential to uncover neurobiological differences between individuals that may influence their learning abilities. Ethical considerations arise in terms of ensuring equity and fairness in educational settings. For example, if neurobiological markers are used to identify students who require additional support, there is a risk of creating labels and perpetuating inequality. It is crucial to strike a balance between using neuroscience insights to inform teaching practices and avoiding the stigmatization or discrimination of certain groups.

Potential Risks of Educational Neuroscience

1. **Misinterpretation and Oversimplification:** There is a risk that educational neuroscience findings may be misinterpreted or oversimplified, leading to misguided educational practices. Neuroscience research is complex, and drawing direct causal links between brain activity and learning outcomes can be challenging.

It is crucial to critically evaluate and contextualize research findings before translating them into classroom practices.

2. **Normalization of Neurodiversity**: Educational neuroscience may inadvertently reinforce the notion that neurotypical brain functioning is superior to neurodiverse profiles. If educational practices solely focus on "normalizing" neurological variations, it may neglect the unique strengths and abilities of neurodiverse learners. It is important to adopt inclusive practices that recognize and celebrate neurodiversity in educational settings.

3. **Unintended Consequences**: The implementation of educational neuroscience findings may have unintended consequences. For example, if brain-based interventions are promoted without sufficient evidence, they could divert resources from other evidence-based approaches. There is also a risk that neuroscientific explanations for educational outcomes may overly simplify the complex interplay between biological and environmental factors.

4. **Commercialization and Privacy Concerns**: As the field of educational neuroscience develops, there is a risk of commercialization, with companies marketing products and interventions based on limited or preliminary research. This raises concerns regarding the efficacy and safety of such interventions. Additionally, commercialization may raise privacy concerns if companies collect and analyze student neurodata without adequate consent or protection.

Case Study: Brain-Computer Interfaces in Education

Brain-computer interfaces (BCIs) are a potential application of educational neuroscience that allows direct communication between the brain and external devices. BCIs have the potential to revolutionize education by enabling students with motor disabilities to control computers or robotic devices using their brain activity.

However, the use of BCIs in education raises ethical considerations and potential risks. For instance, there is a need to ensure informed consent from students and their parents, with clear explanations of the potential benefits and risks associated with BCI technology. Privacy concerns arise when collecting and storing sensitive brain activity data, and measures must be taken to protect the confidentiality of this information. There is also a risk of creating further disparities if BCI technology is not accessible to all students due to financial constraints or limited availability.

To mitigate these risks, ethical guidelines for the use of BCIs in education should be established, ensuring equitable access, informed consent, and privacy protection.

Ongoing monitoring and evaluation of the impact of BCIs in educational settings are essential to ensure that the benefits are maximized and potential risks are minimized.

Conclusion

Educational neuroscience holds immense promise for improving learning and teaching practices. However, it is crucial to address the ethical considerations and potential risks associated with its implementation. By adopting a thoughtful and cautious approach, educational neuroscience can contribute to the development of evidence-based and ethically sound educational practices that positively impact learners.

Subsection 5: Future Directions and Challenges in Educational Neuroscience Research

Educational neuroscience is a rapidly evolving field that seeks to understand the relationship between brain function, learning, and education. As researchers continue to uncover new insights about the brain and its impact on learning processes, the field of educational neuroscience is poised to make significant advancements in the coming years. This section explores the future directions and challenges in educational neuroscience research, shedding light on the potential developments and obstacles that lie ahead.

Future Directions in Educational Neuroscience

1. **Personalized Learning and Brain Profiling:** One of the exciting possibilities in educational neuroscience is the development of brain profiling techniques to inform personalized learning. By studying individual brain patterns, researchers can gain insights into how students process information and tailor instructional strategies to their specific needs. Future research may explore the use of neuroimaging techniques, such as functional magnetic resonance imaging (fMRI) or electroencephalography (EEG), to identify neural signatures associated with different cognitive processes. This information could be used to design personalized interventions and enhance individual learning outcomes.

2. **Neurofeedback Training:** Neurofeedback is a promising technique that allows individuals to monitor and regulate their own brain activity. This approach uses real-time feedback from neuroimaging or electroencephalogram (EEG) devices to teach individuals to self-regulate their brain function. In the future, educational neuroscience research may investigate the use of neurofeedback in educational settings to enhance attention, memory, and self-regulation skills. By

providing students with real-time information about their brain activity, neurofeedback training could help them develop metacognitive strategies and improve their learning abilities.

3.   **Brain-Computer Interfaces (BCIs) in Education:**   Brain-computer interfaces (BCIs) enable direct communication between the brain and external devices, opening up new possibilities for educational applications. As BCIs become more advanced and accessible, future research may explore their potential in enhancing learning and instructional techniques. For example, BCIs could be used to provide real-time feedback on cognitive states, such as attention or engagement, and adapt educational materials accordingly.   Additionally, BCIs could facilitate communication for learners with disabilities by allowing them to interact with educational content using their brain signals.

4.   **Mindfulness and Brain Plasticity:** Mindfulness practices have gained increasing attention for their potential cognitive and emotional benefits. Research has shown that mindfulness training can modify brain structures and enhance cognitive functions, such as attention and self-regulation.   In the future, educational neuroscience may investigate the effects of mindfulness interventions on student learning outcomes and brain plasticity.   Understanding how mindfulness practices influence neural networks involved in learning could lead to the integration of mindfulness-based interventions in educational settings, promoting students' overall well-being and academic success.

Challenges in Educational Neuroscience Research

While the future of educational neuroscience holds immense promise, it also faces certain challenges that need to be addressed for the field to progress effectively. These challenges include:

1.   **Ethical Considerations:** As the field of educational neuroscience embraces techniques such as neuroimaging and brain-computer interfaces, ethical considerations become paramount.   Researchers must grapple with issues surrounding the privacy and consent of participants, especially when working with children.   Clear guidelines and regulations should be developed and implemented to ensure the ethical use of brain data in educational research.

2.   **Multidisciplinary Collaboration:** Educational neuroscience research necessitates collaboration among experts from various disciplines, including neuroscience, psychology, education, and cognitive science.   Building effective interdisciplinary partnerships can be challenging due to the different perspectives, methodologies, and terminologies employed by each field. Future research should

actively encourage collaboration to foster a deeper understanding of the complex relationship between the brain, learning, and education.

3.   **Translation into Practice:**   Bridging the gap between educational neuroscience research and its practical application in educational settings remains a significant challenge.   The translation of research findings into effective teaching strategies and interventions requires a comprehensive understanding of both the neuroscientific and educational principles.   Future research should focus on developing evidence-based practices and establishing effective dissemination channels to ensure that the insights gained from educational neuroscience research make a tangible impact on teaching and learning.

4. **Generalizability of Findings:** Educational neuroscience research typically involves small sample sizes and controlled laboratory settings, which may limit the generalizability of findings to real-world educational contexts.   Future research should strive to include larger and more diverse populations, such as students from different cultural backgrounds and varying socioeconomic statuses. This will help validate the applicability of research findings across a wide range of educational settings and populations.

5. **Keeping Pace With Technological Advancements:** The field of educational neuroscience is heavily influenced by advancements in neuroimaging technologies and data analysis techniques.   As technology continues to evolve rapidly, researchers face the challenge of staying up-to-date with the latest tools and methodologies. Collaborations between researchers and technologists are essential to ensure that educational neuroscience research keeps pace with technological advancements and leverages them effectively to advance our understanding of learning and cognition.

In conclusion, the future of educational neuroscience holds great promise for transforming teaching and learning practices.   Exciting developments such as personalized learning, neurofeedback training, brain-computer interfaces, and mindfulness interventions can enhance educational experiences and optimize student outcomes.   However, addressing ethical considerations, fostering interdisciplinary collaboration, translating research into practice, ensuring generalizability, and keeping pace with technological advancements remain key challenges for researchers in the field.   By overcoming these hurdles, educational neuroscience can continue to shape modern education and contribute to the ongoing improvement of teaching and learning practices.

Section 3: Assessment and Feedback

Subsection 1: Importance of assessment and feedback in the learning process

Assessment and feedback play a crucial role in the learning process, providing valuable information to both learners and educators. They serve as integral components of education, guiding instructional decisions, and promoting student growth and development. In this subsection, we will explore the importance of assessment and feedback and discuss various strategies to enhance their effectiveness.

Assessment: A Tool for Gauging Learning

Assessment is a systematic process of gathering evidence and making judgments about student learning outcomes. It helps educators understand what students know, understand, and can do. Effective assessments provide valuable insights into student progress, instructional effectiveness, and the overall effectiveness of educational programs.

Formative Assessment versus Summative Assessment Assessments can be categorized into two main types: formative and summative. Formative assessment refers to assessments conducted during the learning process to monitor student progress and provide feedback for improvement. It aims to enhance learning by identifying areas of strength and weakness. On the other hand, summative assessment occurs at the end of a unit, course, or program to evaluate student achievement and assign grades or certifications.

Benefits of Assessment Assessment offers numerous benefits to both educators and learners. For educators, it helps in tracking student progress, identifying learning gaps, and adapting instructional strategies accordingly. Through assessment, educators gain insights into their teaching effectiveness and can make informed decisions about curriculum design and content delivery. For learners, assessment provides a clear understanding of their strengths and areas that require improvement. It promotes self-reflection, motivation, and a sense of achievement. Additionally, assessments allow learners to gauge their progress and make informed decisions about future learning goals.

Feedback: A Catalyst for Learning

Feedback is a critical element in the educational process as it helps learners understand how they are performing and how to improve. Effective feedback provides constructive guidance, facilitates self-assessment, and encourages engagement and reflection. It is essential for promoting student growth and meeting learning objectives.

Characteristics of Effective Feedback Effective feedback should be timely, specific, and constructive. It should focus on the task or learning goal, highlight areas for improvement, and suggest ways to enhance performance. Feedback should be clear, concise, and provided in a supportive manner to ensure that learners can understand and apply it.

Functions of Feedback Feedback serves multiple functions in the learning process. Firstly, it provides information to learners about their progress and performance, allowing them to identify their strengths and weaknesses. Secondly, feedback guides learners on how to improve their work by highlighting specific areas for development. It supports the development of metacognitive skills, helping learners become aware of their thinking processes. Lastly, feedback motivates and encourages learners by recognizing their efforts and achievements.

Strategies for Effective Feedback To ensure the effectiveness of feedback, educators should consider several strategies. One approach is to provide feedback that is specific and actionable. Instead of simply stating whether an answer is correct or incorrect, educators should explain why it is so and offer suggestions for improvement. Additionally, feedback should be provided in a timely manner, allowing learners to make immediate connections between their work and the feedback received. Peer feedback and self-assessment can also be integrated into the learning process, encouraging students to take ownership of their learning and providing opportunities for collaboration and reflection.

The Role of Technology in Assessment and Feedback

Technology plays a pivotal role in enhancing assessment and feedback practices in education. It provides innovative tools and platforms that offer new opportunities for data collection, analysis, and communication. Technology-enabled assessments can be more interactive, engaging, and aligned with real-world scenarios.

Furthermore, digital platforms allow for immediate and personalized feedback, enabling learners to track their progress in real-time.

Adaptive Assessment and Personalized Feedback Adaptive assessment is an emerging technology that tailors the assessment experience to the individual learner's needs and abilities. It adapts the difficulty level and content based on the learner's responses, ensuring an optimized learning experience. Personalized feedback, facilitated by technology, provides learners with tailored suggestions, resources, and learning pathways, catering to their specific needs and promoting self-directed learning.

Data Analytics and Learning Analytics Technology enables educators to gather and analyze vast amounts of data related to student performance, learning patterns, and engagement. Data analytics and learning analytics provide valuable insights for educators to identify trends, predict student needs, and make informed decisions about instructional strategies or interventions. These analytics can inform curriculum design, identify areas of improvement, and support evidence-based decision-making.

Conclusion

Assessment and feedback are essential components of the learning process, providing valuable information to both learners and educators. Through effective assessment practices, educators can monitor student progress, identify learning gaps, and adapt instruction to meet individual needs. Feedback, when delivered in a timely and constructive manner, guides learners in their journey towards improvement and promotes self-reflection and growth. Technology enhances assessment and feedback practices, offering adaptive assessment options, personalized feedback, and powerful data analysis tools. By prioritizing assessment and feedback, educators can create a learner-centered environment that fosters student success and engagement.

Subsection 2: Different types of assessments and their uses in education

In education, assessment plays a crucial role in measuring student learning and performance. It provides valuable information to teachers, students, and parents about the progress and achievement of learners. Different types of assessments are used to gather data on various aspects of student learning, including knowledge, skills, understanding, and application. This subsection explores the different types of assessments commonly used in education and their specific uses.

Formative Assessments

Formative assessments are used throughout the learning process to monitor and provide feedback on student progress. These assessments are designed to inform instruction and help students identify areas for improvement. The main purpose of formative assessments is to guide teaching and learning rather than grade students. Examples of formative assessments include quizzes, exit tickets, classroom discussions, and observations.

Formative assessments are valuable tools for teachers to identify students' strengths and weaknesses, adjust instructional strategies, and provide targeted support. They promote active engagement and reflection, allowing students to take ownership of their learning. By using formative assessments, teachers can diagnose misconceptions, plan targeted interventions, and provide timely feedback to students, fostering their growth and improvement.

Summative Assessments

Summative assessments are used to evaluate student learning and assign grades or scores at the end of a unit, course, or academic year. These assessments measure students' overall understanding, knowledge, and skills acquired over a specific period. Examples of summative assessments include final exams, standardized tests, term papers, and projects.

The purpose of summative assessments is to assess the effectiveness of instruction, evaluate students' mastery of content, and determine their readiness for advancement. Summative assessments provide a comprehensive overview of students' achievement and contribute to accountability measures in education. They are often used for grade reporting, college admissions, and educational program evaluations.

Diagnostic Assessments

Diagnostic assessments are used to gather information about students' prior knowledge, skills, and understanding before instruction begins. These assessments help teachers identify students' strengths and weaknesses, address their individual needs, and tailor instruction accordingly. Examples of diagnostic assessments include pre-tests, concept maps, and interviews.

The purpose of diagnostic assessments is to guide instructional planning and differentiate instruction. By assessing students' readiness and preconceptions, teachers can design appropriate learning experiences and provide targeted interventions. Diagnostic assessments also help teachers identify gaps in knowledge and skills, allowing them to scaffold instruction effectively.

Authentic Assessments

Authentic assessments are designed to measure students' ability to apply knowledge and skills in real-world contexts or situations. These assessments focus on the application of knowledge rather than memorization and recall. Examples of authentic assessments include projects, portfolios, simulations, and performances.

The purpose of authentic assessments is to assess students' higher-order thinking skills, problem-solving abilities, and creativity. They provide opportunities for students to demonstrate their understanding and skills in meaningful and relevant ways. Authentic assessments promote critical thinking, collaboration, and communication, preparing students for the challenges and demands of the real world.

Performance Assessments

Performance assessments measure students' ability to demonstrate competencies through structured tasks or activities. These assessments assess students' knowledge, skills, and abilities based on their actual performance. Examples of performance assessments include oral presentations, laboratory experiments, debates, and practical exams.

The purpose of performance assessments is to evaluate students' mastery of specific skills or procedures. They provide a direct measure of students' abilities in practical settings and allow for authentic demonstrations of learning. Performance assessments are particularly valuable in disciplines that require hands-on skills or require students to showcase their capabilities.

Self-Assessments

Self-assessments involve students reflecting on their own learning and assessing their progress against specific criteria. These assessments encourage students to take ownership of their learning and develop metacognitive skills. Examples of self-assessments include self-reflection journals, rubrics, and goal-setting activities.

The purpose of self-assessments is to promote student self-awareness, responsibility, and autonomy. By reflecting on their strengths and areas for growth, students become more actively engaged in the learning process. Self-assessments also help students develop a growth mindset and become lifelong learners.

Peer Assessments

Peer assessments involve students evaluating the work of their peers based on specific criteria or guidelines. These assessments not only provide feedback to the recipient but also develop students' critical thinking and evaluation skills. Examples of peer assessments include peer reviews, group projects with peer evaluations, and collaborative discussions.

The purpose of peer assessments is to foster a collaborative and supportive learning environment where students learn from each other. By engaging in peer assessments, students develop their abilities to evaluate and provide constructive feedback. Peer assessments also promote teamwork, communication skills, and a deeper understanding of the subject matter.

Assessment practices in education should be carefully selected based on the learning goals, instructional context, and assessment purpose. A combination of different assessment types provides a comprehensive and well-rounded view of students' learning and progress. It is important for educators to consider the strengths, limitations, and appropriate uses of each assessment method to make informed decisions that effectively support student learning and growth.

Key Takeaways:

- Formative assessments are used to gather ongoing feedback and guide instruction.

- Summative assessments measure overall learning and assign grades or scores.

- Diagnostic assessments inform instruction by assessing students' prior knowledge and readiness.

- Authentic assessments measure the application of knowledge and skills in real-world contexts.

- Performance assessments assess students' abilities through structured tasks or activities.

- Self-assessments involve students reflecting on their learning and progress.

- Peer assessments involve students evaluating the work of their peers.

In the next section, we will explore strategies for providing effective feedback to enhance learning and the innovations in assessment and feedback practices.

Resources:

+ *Classroom Assessment Techniques: A Handbook for College Teachers* by Thomas A. Angelo and K. Patricia Cross

+ *Transformative Assessment* by W. James Popham

+ *Assessment Essentials: Planning, Implementing, and Improving Assessment in Higher Education* by Catherine M. Wehlburg

Caveat: Assessments should be designed and administered with fairness, validity, and reliability in mind. It is important to consider the diverse needs and backgrounds of students, provide clear instructions and criteria, and ensure the assessment aligns with the intended learning outcomes. Additionally, assessment results should inform instructional decisions and support students' growth rather than solely focusing on grading or ranking.

Subsection 3: Strategies for providing effective feedback to enhance learning

Feedback plays a crucial role in the learning process, as it helps students understand their progress, identify areas for improvement, and reinforce their learning. Effective feedback can enhance learning outcomes and promote student engagement and motivation. In this section, we will discuss strategies for providing high-quality feedback that supports student learning and development.

Principles of Effective Feedback

To provide effective feedback, educators should consider the following principles:

1. **Timeliness:** Feedback should be provided in a timely manner to ensure its relevance and usefulness. Students need feedback while the learning is still fresh in their minds, enabling them to make immediate adjustments and improvements.

2. **Specificity:** Feedback should be clear and specific, focusing on specific learning goals and providing concrete examples. Vague feedback such as "Good job!" may not provide meaningful guidance to students. Instead, feedback should pinpoint areas of strength and areas that need improvement.

3. **Constructiveness:** Feedback should be constructive, emphasizing areas for improvement rather than simply pointing out mistakes or shortcomings. Constructive feedback helps students understand what they need to do differently and offers suggestions or strategies to enhance their learning.

4. **Individualization:** Feedback should take into account individual student needs and learning styles. Personalizing feedback can help students feel valued and supported, increasing their motivation and engagement in the learning process.

5. **Goal-oriented:** Feedback should be tied to specific learning goals and objectives. It should clarify how students are progressing towards these goals and what steps they can take to further their learning. By aligning feedback with learning objectives, students can better understand their learning trajectory.

6. **Self-reflective:** Feedback should encourage self-reflection and metacognition. Students should be prompted to evaluate their own work, identify strengths and areas for improvement, and develop strategies for further learning. Self-reflective feedback fosters a deeper understanding of one's own learning process.

Strategies for Providing Feedback

To provide effective feedback that enhances learning, educators can employ various strategies. Let's explore some of these strategies:

1. **Written Comments:** Providing written comments on assignments, tests, or projects is a common way to give feedback. When providing written feedback, it is important to be specific, focusing on strengths and areas for improvement. Pointing out specific examples or giving suggestions for improvement can make the feedback more actionable for students. It is also helpful to offer praise and encouragement to motivate students.

   Example: "Great job on your essay! Your argumentation was well-supported with evidence from credible sources. To improve further, consider organizing your paragraphs more effectively by providing clear topic sentences and using transitional words to enhance coherence."

2. **Rubrics and Checklists:** Using rubrics or checklists can provide clear criteria for assessment and feedback. Rubrics outline the expectations for

different aspects of an assignment, enabling students to self-assess their work and understand the feedback they receive. Checklists can be useful for providing feedback on specific tasks or skills.

Example: "Here is a rubric outlining the criteria we used to assess your presentation. It includes categories such as content, organization, delivery, and visual aids. Use the rubric to reflect on your performance, identifying areas where you excel and areas where you can improve for future presentations."

3. **Verbal Feedback:** Providing verbal feedback through one-on-one discussions, in-person or virtual meetings, or audio recordings can be highly valuable. Verbal feedback allows for immediate clarification, encourages dialogue, and enables personalized guidance. It also allows educators to offer tone, intonation, and gestures that can enhance the understanding and delivery of feedback.

Example: "I noticed that you struggled with the pronunciation of some words during your presentation. Let's work on that together. I suggest practicing those words with a native speaker or using online pronunciation resources. Keep up the great work with your content and delivery!"

4. **Peer Feedback:** Encouraging students to provide feedback to their peers can promote a collaborative learning environment and develop critical thinking and communication skills. Peer feedback can take the form of structured feedback forms, group discussions, or peer-editing sessions.

Example: "In pairs, exchange your essays and provide feedback to each other using these guiding questions. Focus on clarity of arguments, evidence, and organization. Make sure to offer constructive suggestions for improvement. Share your feedback with your partner and engage in a discussion about how to enhance the quality of each other's work."

5. **Technology-Enabled Feedback:** Leveraging technology can provide innovative ways to deliver feedback. Digital tools such as annotation software, online discussion boards, or video feedback platforms can enhance the feedback experience. Technology can enable multimedia feedback with audio or video recordings, allowing for more personalized and detailed guidance.

Example: "I have recorded a screencast video of myself reviewing your code. In the video, I demonstrated some optimizations you could make to improve its efficiency. Watch the video, take notes, and feel free to ask any questions or seek clarification."

Potential Challenges and Tips

Providing effective feedback can be challenging for educators. Here are some common challenges and tips to overcome them:

+ **Time constraints:** Time limitations make it difficult to provide detailed feedback on every aspect of a student's work. Focus on the most critical areas for improvement and provide specific examples or suggestions to guide students.

+ **Overwhelming feedback:** Providing an overwhelming amount of feedback can be counterproductive and lead to student confusion or frustration. Prioritize and highlight a few key points for improvement, focusing on achievable goals and actionable steps.

+ **Balancing positive and constructive feedback:** It is essential to strike a balance between positive reinforcement and constructive criticism. Recognize students' strengths and accomplishments while providing guidance for improvement.

+ **Addressing diverse student needs:** Different students may have varying learning styles, abilities, and preferences for receiving feedback. Consider individualizing the feedback approach to cater to diverse student needs, ensuring it is accessible and meaningful for all.

+ **Promoting feedback acceptance:** Students may be resistant to feedback or perceive it as judgment. Foster a supportive and non-threatening environment that encourages students to embrace feedback as an opportunity for growth and learning.

Summary

Providing effective feedback is essential for enhancing student learning and development. By following the principles of timeliness, specificity, constructiveness, individualization, goal-orientation, and self-reflection, educators can create meaningful feedback experiences for students. Strategies such as written comments, rubrics and checklists, verbal feedback, peer feedback, and technology-enabled feedback can be employed to deliver feedback effectively.

Overcoming challenges related to time constraints, overwhelming feedback, balancing positivity and constructive elements, addressing diverse student needs, and promoting feedback acceptance can further improve the feedback process. With careful consideration and implementation of these strategies, educators can enhance the impact of feedback on students' learning outcomes and foster a culture of continuous improvement.

Subsection 4: Innovations in Assessment and Feedback Practices

Assessment and feedback are integral components of the learning process. They are essential for both teachers and learners to gauge progress, identify areas for improvement, and promote continuous growth. Traditional assessment methods, such as exams and quizzes, have their limitations and may not effectively capture the full extent of a student's skills and knowledge. Therefore, it is crucial to explore and utilize innovative assessment and feedback practices that provide a more comprehensive and personalized approach to evaluating student learning. In this subsection, we will discuss some of the latest advancements in assessment and feedback techniques, their benefits, and how they can be effectively implemented in educational settings.

Formative Assessment

Formative assessment is an approach that emphasizes providing ongoing feedback and support to students throughout the learning process. Unlike summative assessment, which occurs at the end of a unit or course, formative assessment aims to identify student strengths and weaknesses in real-time, allowing for timely adjustments to instruction.

One innovation in formative assessment is the use of technology. Digital tools, such as online quizzes, interactive simulations, and educational games, enable teachers to gather immediate feedback on student performance and tailor instruction accordingly. For example, online platforms like Kahoot! and Quizlet Live allow teachers to create engaging quizzes that provide instant feedback to students. These tools not only make assessment more interactive and enjoyable but also facilitate data collection for further analysis.

Another innovative approach to formative assessment is peer assessment. In this method, students are actively involved in assessing their peers' work based on predetermined criteria. Peer assessment not only encourages self-reflection and critical thinking but also promotes a deeper understanding of the subject matter. Digital platforms, like Google Docs or Peergrade, can facilitate the smooth implementation of peer assessment by streamlining the feedback process and ensuring anonymity.

Performance-Based Assessment

Performance-based assessment focuses on evaluating students' ability to apply their knowledge and skills in real-world situations. It goes beyond traditional pen-and-paper tests by requiring students to demonstrate their understanding through authentic tasks, such as projects, presentations, or simulations.

One innovative approach to performance-based assessment is project-based assessment. This method involves students working on a complex, real-world project that requires them to apply multiple skills and knowledge from different subject areas. For example, a project on sustainable energy might require students to analyze data, propose solutions, and present their findings. Project-based assessment not only assesses students' understanding but also enhances their problem-solving, collaboration, and communication skills.

Another innovative technique is portfolio assessment, which involves collecting and evaluating a collection of a student's work samples over time. Portfolios can include various forms of evidence, such as written assignments, artwork, or multimedia presentations. This approach provides a more holistic view of a student's progress and allows for self-reflection on personal growth and achievements.

Adaptive Assessment

Adaptive assessment leverages technology to tailor the assessment experience to each individual student's needs. Through the use of algorithms, adaptive assessment platforms can adjust the difficulty of questions based on students' responses, providing a personalized and optimized assessment experience.

One example of adaptive assessment is computer-adaptive testing (CAT). CAT uses a bank of questions with varying levels of difficulty, and the computer selects subsequent questions based on the student's previous responses. If a student answers a question correctly, the system presents a more challenging question, while an incorrect answer leads to an easier question. This adaptive approach allows for more efficient and accurate assessment of students' knowledge and skills compared to traditional fixed-question tests.

Another innovative form of adaptive assessment is game-based assessment. Gamification elements, such as leaderboards, achievements, and rewards, are incorporated into the assessment process to engage students and motivate them to perform their best. Platforms like Classcraft and Prodigy seamlessly integrate educational content with game mechanics, making assessment a fun and immersive experience.

Multimodal Feedback

Feedback is a crucial component of the assessment process, providing students with information on their performance and guiding them toward improvement. Multimodal feedback involves providing feedback through various channels, such as written comments, audio recordings, or video annotations.

One innovation in multimodal feedback is screencasting. Using screen capture technology, teachers can record their computer screen while providing verbal feedback on students' work. This approach allows for more detailed and personalized feedback, as teachers can highlight specific areas, explain concepts visually, and address common misconceptions in real-time. Tools like Screencast-O-Matic and Loom make it easy for teachers to create and share screencasts with their students.

Another innovative approach is peer feedback using video annotations. Students can record themselves providing feedback on their peers' work while annotating specific parts of the assignment. This method promotes active engagement with the material and encourages students to think critically about their own understanding and the work of their peers. Digital platforms like VideoAnt and VoiceThread facilitate the integration of video-based peer feedback into the assessment process.

In conclusion, innovations in assessment and feedback practices have the potential to revolutionize the way we evaluate learning and provide meaningful support to students. By incorporating formative assessment, performance-based assessment, adaptive assessment, and multimodal feedback, teachers can create a more engaging, personalized, and effective learning environment. It is essential for educators to embrace these innovations and explore their potential to enhance student achievement, foster a growth mindset, and promote lifelong learning.

Subsection 5: Addressing challenges and ensuring fairness in assessment

Assessment plays a crucial role in education by providing valuable feedback to students and informing instructional decisions. However, in order for assessment to be effective, it needs to address various challenges and ensure fairness for all learners. In this section, we will explore some of the common challenges faced in assessment and discuss strategies to promote fairness in the assessment process.

Challenges in assessment

1. **Bias in assessment:** One of the significant challenges in assessment is the potential for bias, which can occur due to various factors such as cultural differences, socioeconomic status, or stereotypes. Bias in assessment can lead to unfair outcomes and may disadvantage certain groups of students. It is essential to address bias and ensure that assessments are fair and free from any form of discrimination.

2. **Validity and reliability:** Assessment validity refers to the extent to which an assessment measures what it intends to measure, while reliability is about the consistency and accuracy of the assessment results. Ensuring validity and reliability in assessment can be challenging, as it requires careful design and alignment with learning objectives. Without valid and reliable assessments, the feedback provided might not accurately represent students' knowledge and skills.

3. **Standardization and differentiation:** Balancing the need for standardized assessments and individualized differentiation can be a challenge. On one hand, standardized assessments provide a consistent measure across a group of students, allowing for comparisons and monitoring progress. On the other hand, differentiating assessments based on students' diverse needs ensures fair opportunities for all learners. Striking the right balance between standardization and differentiation is crucial to address the challenges in assessment.

4. **Assessment overload:** With the increasing focus on accountability and measuring educational outcomes, there is a risk of assessment overload. Students can experience high levels of stress and anxiety when faced with excessive assessments. Moreover, frequent assessments might not provide enough time for deep learning and reflection. Managing and reducing assessment overload is essential for promoting fair and effective assessment practices.

Strategies for ensuring fairness in assessment

1. **Clear assessment criteria and rubrics:** Providing students with clear assessment criteria and rubrics can help eliminate ambiguity and ensure transparency in the assessment process. Clearly defining the expectations and standards allows students to understand how they will be assessed and what they need to do to succeed. This approach helps promote fairness by ensuring that all students are assessed against the same criteria.

2. **Multiple forms of assessment:** Relying on a single form of assessment may not capture the diverse skills and abilities of all students. Incorporating multiple forms of assessment, such as written assignments, presentations, group work, and

practical tasks, can provide a more comprehensive view of students' capabilities. Using a variety of assessment methods accommodates different learning styles and allows students to showcase their strengths in different areas.

3. **Addressing bias:** It is essential to address and minimize bias in assessment. This can be done by critically examining assessment materials and items to ensure they are free from cultural, gender, or socioeconomic biases. Additionally, providing diverse examples and contexts in assessment tasks can help reduce bias and promote inclusivity. Training teachers and assessors on identifying and eliminating bias is also crucial for fair assessment practices.

4. **Promoting assessment literacy:** Educating students about assessment processes, including the purpose, criteria, and expectations, can empower them to become active participants in their own learning. By promoting assessment literacy, students can understand how assessments align with their learning goals and take ownership of their learning progress. Assessment literacy also includes teaching students how to give and receive constructive feedback, promoting a growth mindset, and fostering a culture of continuous improvement.

5. **Flexible assessment options:** Providing flexible assessment options allows students with diverse needs to demonstrate their learning in ways that are accessible and meaningful to them. For example, allowing students to choose between a written essay or an oral presentation caters to different learning preferences and strengths. Flexibility in assessment also considers students with disabilities or language barriers, ensuring fair opportunities for all learners.

Case Study: Implementing fair assessment in mathematics

In a mathematics classroom, fair assessment can be challenging due to the subject's objective nature. However, by adopting inclusive practices and addressing biases, teachers can promote fairness in mathematics assessment. Here is an example:

Challenge: In a diverse classroom, the teacher wants to ensure that the mathematics assessment is fair and impartial, considering the students' cultural backgrounds and language proficiency.

Solution: The teacher designs an assessment task that incorporates real-life examples and contexts that reflect the cultural diversity of the students. The task requires students to apply mathematical concepts to solve problems related to their own cultural experiences. By doing so, the teacher not only engages students but also ensures that the assessment is relevant and meaningful to all learners. Additionally, the teacher provides comprehensive rubrics and exemplars to guide students' understanding of expectations and facilitate self-assessment.

This approach allows students to showcase their mathematical skills while honoring their cultural backgrounds, promoting fairness in assessment.

Conclusion

Addressing the challenges and ensuring fairness in assessment is crucial for promoting effective learning and providing equal opportunities for all students. By implementing strategies such as clear assessment criteria, multiple forms of assessment, addressing bias, promoting assessment literacy, and providing flexible assessment options, educators can create a fair and inclusive assessment environment. It is imperative to continuously reflect on assessment practices and adapt them to meet the needs of diverse learners, fostering a culture of fairness and growth.

Chapter 4: Case Studies in Educational Success

Section 1: K-12 Education

Subsection 1: Success Stories in Elementary Education

Elementary education plays a crucial role in shaping young minds and providing them with a strong foundation for future learning. In this subsection, we will explore some inspiring success stories in elementary education that highlight effective teaching strategies, innovative programs, and positive outcomes for students.

Story 1: The Power of Multisensory Learning

One success story in elementary education revolves around the implementation of multisensory learning approaches. In a school district in Michigan, teachers began incorporating hands-on activities, visual aids, and interactive materials into their lessons to engage students and enhance their learning experience.

For example, in a mathematics class, students were introduced to the concept of fractions using a multisensory approach. They used fraction manipulatives, such as fraction bars and circles, to explore the concept through tactile and visual means. They also engaged in group activities where they divided objects into equal parts and discussed their findings. This multisensory approach not only helped students understand the concept of fractions more effectively, but also increased their motivation and engagement in the learning process.

The success of this approach was evident in improved student performance. Students showed a significant increase in their understanding of fractions, as well as higher levels of confidence and enthusiasm in mathematics. Moreover, the multisensory approach benefited students with different learning styles, allowing them to grasp the concept in a way that resonated with their individual strengths.

Story 2: Cultivating a Growth Mindset

Another success story in elementary education involves the implementation of a growth mindset framework. In a school district in California, teachers adopted a growth mindset approach to empower students and foster a love for learning.

Teachers dedicated time to explicitly teach students about the concept of a growth mindset, emphasizing that intelligence and abilities can be developed through effort and perseverance. They encouraged students to embrace challenges, view mistakes as opportunities for growth, and cultivate a positive attitude towards learning.

To reinforce the growth mindset philosophy, teachers provided regular feedback and praised students' efforts and strategies rather than focusing solely on their achievements. They created a nurturing classroom environment where students felt comfortable taking risks and where their mistakes were seen as valuable learning experiences.

The impact of this approach was remarkable. Students developed resilience and a strong belief in their ability to improve. They tackled challenging tasks with enthusiasm and displayed a willingness to seek help and explore different strategies. As a result, both academic performance and self-confidence significantly increased among the students.

Story 3: Engaging Parents as Partners in Education

The involvement of parents in elementary education is essential for a child's success. In a school district in Texas, a program was implemented to actively engage parents as partners in their children's education.

Teachers organized regular parent-teacher conferences to discuss students' progress and set academic goals. They also provided parents with resources and strategies to support learning at home. In addition, the school hosted workshops and events where parents could learn about various aspects of their child's education, such as effective study habits, positive discipline strategies, and the importance of reading.

By fostering a strong partnership between parents and educators, students benefited from consistent support and guidance both at school and at home. The program resulted in improved student attendance, higher levels of parental involvement, and increased academic achievement.

Story 4: Integrating Nature and Outdoor Education

Recognizing the importance of connecting children with nature, a school in Oregon implemented an outdoor education program. The program aimed to provide students with hands-on learning experiences in natural environments, fostering a sense of wonder, curiosity, and environmental stewardship.

Teachers incorporated outdoor activities and explorations into their curriculum, allowing students to engage with nature in meaningful ways. They utilized local parks, gardens, and natural areas as classrooms, where students learned about ecological concepts, conducted experiments, and participated in conservation projects.

The positive impact of this program was evident in various aspects of students' development. They showed increased attentiveness, creativity, and problem-solving skills. They also displayed a heightened sense of responsibility towards the environment and developed a stronger connection with their surroundings.

Story 5: Embracing Cultural Diversity

In a school district in New York, educators implemented a culturally responsive teaching approach to honor and celebrate the diverse backgrounds and experiences of their students. Teachers actively sought to create an inclusive classroom environment that recognized and respected cultural differences.

They integrated culturally diverse literature and materials into their lessons, ensuring that students could see themselves reflected in the curriculum. Teachers also encouraged students to share their unique cultural perspectives and experiences, fostering a sense of belonging and identity.

The impact of this approach was profound. Students developed a deeper appreciation for cultural diversity, gained a better understanding of their own heritage, and developed empathy and respect for others. The classroom became a vibrant and inclusive space where students felt valued and understood.

These success stories in elementary education illustrate the power of innovative teaching approaches, partnerships with families, and a focus on individual needs and interests. By adopting these practices and adapting them to their own contexts, educators can create positive and transformative learning experiences for elementary students.

Subsection 2: Innovative Practices in Middle School Education

Middle school education is a critical phase in a student's academic journey, where they transition from elementary school to high school. This period is characterized by significant physical, emotional, and cognitive changes in students, making it essential to adopt innovative practices that cater to their unique needs. In this subsection, we will explore some innovative practices in middle school education that promote engagement, motivation, and successful learning outcomes.

Creating a Personalized Learning Environment

One innovative practice in middle school education is the creation of a personalized learning environment. Personalized learning recognizes that each student has unique learning preferences, interests, and strengths. By tailoring instruction to meet individual needs, educators can foster deeper engagement and improve academic outcomes.

A key aspect of personalized learning is providing students with opportunities to make choices and take ownership of their learning. Teachers can offer a range of assignments or project options that align with the curriculum objectives, allowing students to select topics that resonate with their interests. This choice empowers students and enhances their motivation to learn.

Another element of personalized learning is the incorporation of technology. Middle school students are digital natives, and technology can be used to enhance their learning experience. For example, online platforms and digital tools can provide adaptive learning modules that adjust the curriculum to a student's proficiency level. This allows students to work at their own pace, filling knowledge gaps and advancing in areas where they excel.

Example: In a middle school science class, students are learning about renewable energy sources. The teacher gives them the option to choose a specific energy source they want to research further. Students can create presentations, design models, or conduct experiments to showcase their understanding of the chosen energy source. By providing choice and leveraging technology, the teacher promotes personalized learning and encourages active engagement.

Incorporating Project-Based Learning (PBL)

Project-based learning (PBL) is an innovative approach that promotes active, hands-on learning experiences in the middle school classroom. This method focuses on student-centered projects that allow students to explore real-world problems and develop critical thinking, collaboration, and problem-solving skills.

In a PBL setting, teachers act as facilitators, guiding students through the project process. Students are given an authentic problem or challenge and are encouraged to investigate, analyze, and propose solutions. This approach fosters creativity, independence, and a deeper understanding of the subject matter.

To implement PBL effectively, teachers should scaffold the project process by breaking it down into manageable steps. Clear guidelines and objectives should be provided, along with checkpoints to track progress. Additionally, teachers should incorporate opportunities for peer collaboration and feedback, encouraging students to reflect on their work and make improvements.

Example: In a middle school social studies class, students are studying various civilizations throughout history. The teacher assigns a project where students must research and create a museum exhibit on a specific civilization. Students work in teams, conducting research, designing exhibits, and presenting their findings to the class. This project-based approach fosters research skills, teamwork, and presentation skills, making the learning experience more meaningful and engaging.

Promoting Experiential Learning

Middle school students thrive when they can connect their learning to the real world. Promoting experiential learning is an innovative practice that enables students to apply their knowledge and skills in practical contexts, enhancing their understanding and retention of concepts.

Experiential learning can take various forms, such as field trips, service-learning projects, simulations, or role-playing activities. By immersing students in authentic experiences, educators can create meaningful connections between academic content and real-world situations.

Teachers can also invite guest speakers or experts from relevant fields to share their experiences and insights with students. This exposure to real-world professionals can inspire and motivate students, helping them see the relevance and application of their learning.

Example: In a middle school language arts class, students are studying a historical fiction novel set during World War II. The teacher arranges a field trip to a local history museum, where students can see artifacts, documents, and exhibitions related to the time period. Students engage in guided discussions and activities to connect the events in the novel to the historical context. This experiential learning opportunity enhances their understanding of the novel and the historical period.

Integrating Multimodal Learning Strategies

Middle school students have diverse learning preferences and strengths. Integrating multimodal learning strategies acknowledges these differences and provides students with multiple ways to access and engage with the curriculum.

Multimodal learning involves presenting information through various formats, such as text, images, videos, audio, and interactive activities. This approach recognizes that different students may learn better through visual, auditory, or kinesthetic means. By offering a range of learning modalities, educators can support different learning styles and enhance comprehension and retention.

Teachers can utilize technology tools to integrate multimodal learning strategies. For example, they can create multimedia presentations, use educational videos, or provide interactive online activities. Additionally, hands-on activities and group discussions can cater to students who prefer kinesthetic or auditory learning.

Example: In a middle school mathematics class, students are learning about geometric shapes and their properties. The teacher incorporates a multimodal approach by providing visual aids, such as diagrams and 3D models, auditory explanations, and interactive online simulations. Students can choose the mode that best suits their learning style and engage in activities that reinforce their understanding of geometric concepts.

Addressing Social and Emotional Development

Middle school is a crucial time for social and emotional development. Innovative practices in middle school education address the social and emotional needs of students, fostering a positive and supportive learning environment.

One approach is to implement social-emotional learning (SEL) programs that explicitly teach students skills for self-awareness, self-management, social awareness, relationship-building, and responsible decision-making. These programs promote emotional intelligence, resilience, and empathy among students, enhancing their overall well-being and academic success.

In addition, creating a sense of belonging and community within the classroom is essential. Teachers can facilitate team-building activities, collaborative group projects, and open discussions that promote inclusivity and respect for diversity. By valuing students' unique perspectives and experiences, educators create a safe and supportive space for learning.

Example: In a middle school health class, the teacher incorporates a social-emotional learning program into the curriculum. Students engage in activities that promote self-reflection, empathy, and effective communication. The class also includes regular discussions on topics such as bullying prevention, managing stress, and building positive relationships. These practices support the social and emotional well-being of students, creating a positive classroom environment.

Conclusion

Innovative practices in middle school education can significantly enhance student engagement, motivation, and learning outcomes. By personalizing instruction, incorporating project-based learning, promoting experiential learning, integrating multimodal strategies, and addressing social and emotional development, educators can create a dynamic and effective educational experience for middle school students. These practices empower students, foster critical thinking and problem-solving skills, and prepare them for a successful transition to high school and beyond.

Subsection 3: High school success stories and strategies

In this section, we will explore some inspiring success stories and effective strategies that have been implemented in high schools to promote educational success. These stories highlight innovative approaches and practical techniques that have proven to be successful in enhancing student engagement, motivation, and achievement in high school settings.

Story 1: Project-based Learning at Greenfield High School

Greenfield High School is a public high school located in a rural area. In recent years, the school has gained recognition for its successful implementation of project-based learning (PBL). This approach has transformed the learning experience for students, making it more interactive and engaging.

The school's science department designed a project-based unit on sustainability. Students were divided into teams and given the task of creating a sustainable garden on the school premises. They had to research and design the garden, choose appropriate plants, create a budget, and implement their plan.

Through this project, students developed a deeper understanding of sustainable practices, teamwork, and problem-solving skills. They also had the opportunity to apply their knowledge in a real-world context. The project resulted in the creation of a beautiful garden that became a source of pride for the students and the entire school community.

Story 2: Career Pathway Programs at Franklin High School

Franklin High School, located in an urban area, has implemented career pathway programs to provide students with practical skills and knowledge related to specific career fields. These programs offer students the opportunity to explore their interests and gain real-world experience before entering college or the workforce.

One successful pathway program at Franklin High is the Culinary Arts program. Students in this program have the opportunity to learn culinary skills, work in a fully equipped kitchen, and gain experience through internships at local restaurants. The program has not only provided students with valuable practical skills but has also helped them develop a passion for the culinary arts.

Another popular pathway program at Franklin High is the Engineering program. Students in this program have access to state-of-the-art technology and participate in hands-on projects that require engineering principles. This program has not only fostered a love for engineering but has also prepared students for future careers in the field.

These career pathway programs at Franklin High have proven to be successful in preparing students for their future careers by providing them with relevant skills and knowledge. They have also helped students develop a passion for their chosen fields and fostered a sense of purpose and direction.

Strategy 1: Personalized Learning Plans

Personalized learning plans have gained recognition as an effective strategy for promoting educational success in high schools. These plans are tailored to meet the unique needs, interests, and learning styles of individual students. By allowing students to have agency and ownership over their learning, personalized learning plans promote engagement, motivation, and academic growth.

The key components of personalized learning plans include:

- ◆ Goal-setting: Students work with teachers to set specific, measurable, achievable, relevant, and time-bound (SMART) goals.

- ◆ Individual learning pathways: Students have the flexibility to choose learning activities and resources that align with their goals and interests.

- ◆ Regular progress monitoring: Teachers closely monitor students' progress and provide ongoing feedback and support.

- ◆ Flexible pacing: Students have the freedom to learn at their own pace, allowing for mastery of content before progressing to new topics.

+ Differentiated instruction: Teachers use a variety of instructional strategies and resources to meet the diverse needs of students.

Research has shown that personalized learning plans can lead to improved academic performance, increased student engagement, and enhanced self-efficacy. By tailoring the learning experience to each student's needs and interests, high schools can create a more inclusive and empowering learning environment.

Strategy 2: Peer Mentoring Programs

Peer mentoring programs have emerged as a valuable strategy for promoting educational success in high schools. These programs pair older students with younger students to provide academic and social support. Peer mentors serve as role models and provide guidance, encouragement, and assistance to their mentees.

The benefits of peer mentoring programs include:

+ Academic support: Peer mentors can help younger students with homework, study strategies, and subject-specific challenges.

+ Social and emotional support: Peer mentors serve as a source of encouragement, helping mentees navigate the social and emotional challenges of high school.

+ Increased engagement: Peer mentors can inspire mentees to actively participate in school activities and take ownership of their learning.

+ Improved self-confidence: Mentees may develop greater self-confidence and belief in their abilities through positive interactions with their mentors.

One successful example of a peer mentoring program is the "Buddy System" implemented at Ridgeway High School. In this program, senior students are paired with incoming freshmen to provide guidance and support during their transition to high school. The program has been instrumental in reducing the dropout rate and enhancing the overall success of freshmen.

It is important for high schools to establish clear guidelines and training for peer mentors to ensure the effectiveness and safety of the program. By harnessing the power of peer relationships, high schools can create a supportive and collaborative learning environment.

Resource: The Alliance for Excellent Education

The Alliance for Excellent Education is a national policy and advocacy organization dedicated to ensuring that all students graduate from high school prepared for success in college, work, and citizenship. Their website (www.all4ed.org) provides a wealth of resources, research, and tools for improving educational outcomes in high schools. Educators and administrators can access reports, webinars, and guides that offer practical strategies and best practices for high school success.

Key Takeaways

In this section, we explored two inspiring high school success stories and two effective strategies for promoting educational success in high schools. The stories highlighted the transformative impact of project-based learning and career pathway programs. The strategies discussed, personalized learning plans and peer mentoring programs, emphasized the importance of tailoring education to individual student needs and promoting social support within the school community.

By implementing these strategies and learning from successful stories, high schools can create an environment that fosters engagement, motivation, and achievement for all students. With a focus on practical strategies and evidence-based practices, high schools can ensure that students are prepared for success in college, careers, and beyond.

Subsection 4: Addressing Equity and Diversity in K-12 Education

Addressing equity and diversity in K-12 education is of utmost importance in creating an inclusive and fair learning environment for all students. This subsection explores the challenges associated with promoting equity and diversity in educational settings and provides strategies and best practices to address these issues effectively.

Understanding Equity and Diversity in Education

Equity in education refers to ensuring that all students have equal opportunities to succeed and reach their fullest potential, regardless of their background, race, ethnicity, socioeconomic status, or abilities. On the other hand, diversity in education highlights the importance of valuing and embracing differences among students, including their cultural backgrounds, languages, religions, and perspectives. Both equity and diversity are essential for creating a truly inclusive educational environment.

Educators play a vital role in addressing equity and diversity in K-12 education. They need to be conscious of their own biases and actively work to provide equal opportunities for all students, irrespective of their backgrounds. By recognizing and valuing diversity, educators can foster an environment where every student feels respected and included.

Strategies for Promoting Equity and Diversity

Promoting equity and diversity in K-12 education requires a multifaceted approach that involves educators, administrators, policymakers, and the wider community. Here are some strategies that can be implemented to address these issues effectively:

1.   **Culturally Responsive Teaching:**   Culturally responsive teaching encompasses recognizing and incorporating students' cultural backgrounds and experiences into the classroom. Educators can achieve this by integrating diverse perspectives, incorporating culturally relevant materials and resources, and incorporating student voice into the curriculum. For example, when teaching history, educators can provide multiple perspectives on historical events to break away from a single narrative.

2. **Inclusive Curriculum and Pedagogy:** Creating an inclusive curriculum and pedagogy involves ensuring that the materials and teaching methods reflect diversity. Educators can incorporate literature, textbooks, and resources that represent diverse cultures, histories, and experiences. Additionally, instructional strategies should be student-centered, allowing for different learning styles and accommodating diverse abilities.

3.   **Professional Development for Educators:**   Continuous professional development plays a crucial role in equipping educators with the knowledge and skills needed to foster equity and diversity in the classroom. Schools and districts should provide ongoing training and resources to help educators develop a deeper understanding of cultural competence, implicit bias, and strategies for promoting equity in education.

4. **Engaging Families and Communities:** Building strong connections with families and communities is essential for promoting equity and diversity in K-12 education. Schools can engage families by organizing cultural events, family nights, and community partnerships that celebrate and embrace diverse cultures and perspectives.   By involving families and communities, schools can create a supportive network that reinforces the importance of equity and diversity.

Case Studies on Addressing Equity and Diversity

To illustrate the strategies mentioned above, let's explore two case studies highlighting successful initiatives that address equity and diversity in K-12 education:

Case Study 1: Culturally Responsive Curriculum

In a diverse urban school district, educators recognized the need to address cultural relevance in their curriculum. They implemented a culturally responsive curriculum that incorporated literature, historical narratives, and real-world examples that reflected the students' multicultural backgrounds. By incorporating diverse perspectives and experiences into the curriculum, students felt more connected to the learning materials, fostering a sense of belonging and inclusivity. This initiative resulted in increased student engagement, academic achievement, and a positive classroom environment.

Case Study 2: Family and Community Engagement

A suburban elementary school noticed a lack of parent involvement from non-English speaking families. To address this, they implemented a family engagement program that focused on building connections with the diverse community. The program included bilingual workshops, cultural celebrations, and mentorship programs, all aimed at bridging the communication and cultural gap between the school and families. As a result, parents felt more welcomed and valued, leading to increased participation in school activities and improved student outcomes.

Challenges and Future Directions

While progress has been made in addressing equity and diversity in K-12 education, several challenges persist. Some of these challenges include:

- Limited resources and funding to implement comprehensive equity initiatives.

- Implicit bias and stereotypes that can unconsciously impact decision-making processes.

- The need for systemic changes in educational policies and practices to ensure long-term equity.

- The importance of sustained community partnerships and involvement in promoting equity.

To overcome these challenges, ongoing efforts are required to implement evidence-based practices, provide professional development opportunities, and advocate for policies that promote equity and diversity in education. Schools and educators need to continuously evaluate their practices and seek innovative solutions to create inclusive learning environments.

Conclusion

Addressing equity and diversity in K-12 education is a vital aspect of creating inclusive and supportive learning environments. By implementing strategies such as culturally responsive teaching, inclusive curriculum and pedagogy, professional development for educators, and engaging families and communities, schools can foster environments where every student feels valued and included. While challenges exist, a continuous commitment to promoting equity and diversity will lead to positive and transformative changes in K-12 education.

Subsection 5: Future directions and challenges in K-12 education

The landscape of education is continually evolving, influenced by new technologies, changing perspectives on teaching and learning, and the needs of an increasingly diverse student population. In this subsection, we will explore some of the future directions and challenges in K-12 education, discussing key trends and issues that educators, policymakers, and stakeholders should consider.

Future Directions

1. **Personalized Learning Continues to Evolve:** Personalized learning has gained significant attention in recent years, as it allows educators to tailor instruction to individual student needs and interests. In the future, we can expect further advancements in personalized learning approaches, including the use of adaptive technologies, artificial intelligence, and learning analytics to provide even more targeted and customized learning experiences. These innovations will enable students to have greater control over their learning and promote self-directed and lifelong learning skills.

2. **Integration of STEAM Education:** Science, Technology, Engineering, Arts, and Mathematics (STEAM) education is gaining traction as an interdisciplinary approach to learning that prepares students for the demands of a rapidly changing world. In the future, we can expect to see increased emphasis on integrating artistic and creative elements into traditional STEM subjects, fostering

innovation, problem-solving skills, and creativity among students. This integration will nurture the next generation of critical thinkers and innovators.

3. **Embracing Culturally Responsive Education:** As our society becomes more diverse, it is crucial for educators to embrace culturally responsive education, which acknowledges and values the experiences, cultures, and backgrounds of all students. In the future, we can expect to see a greater focus on integrating diverse perspectives, histories, and languages into the curriculum, creating inclusive learning environments where all students feel represented and engaged.

4. **Democratizing Access to Education:** The digital age has transformed the way we access information and learn. In the future, advances in technology will continue to democratize access to education, breaking down barriers to learning and expanding opportunities for students regardless of their geographical location or socioeconomic background. Online platforms, open educational resources, and mobile learning applications will play a significant role in providing equitable educational opportunities to all students.

Challenges

1. **Bridging the Achievement Gap:** Despite efforts to reduce disparities in educational outcomes, the achievement gap between different student groups persists. In the future, addressing this challenge will require a comprehensive approach that focuses on providing targeted support to disadvantaged students, promoting cultural competence among educators, and implementing evidence-based strategies for narrowing the achievement gap. Collaboration between schools, families, and communities will be crucial in creating a more equitable education system.

2. **Balancing Technology Integration:** While technology has the potential to enhance teaching and learning experiences, its integration into classrooms presents challenges. In the future, educators will need to find a delicate balance between incorporating technology and maintaining meaningful human interactions. They will need to navigate issues such as screen time, digital distractions, and the potential for increased inequality if access to technology is not equitable across all student populations.

3. **Preparing Students for an Uncertain Future:** As the world becomes increasingly complex and unpredictable, K-12 education must prepare students for future careers that may not even exist yet. In the future, educators will face the challenge of equipping students with the skills and competencies needed to navigate a rapidly changing job market. This includes a focus on critical thinking, problem-solving, collaboration, adaptability, and digital literacy.

4.   **Redefining Assessment and Accountability:** Traditional models of assessment and accountability, focused primarily on standardized testing, are under scrutiny.   In the future, there will be a shift toward more holistic and authentic forms of assessment that go beyond testing to capture students' diverse skills and talents.   Educators will also need to embrace ongoing and formative assessment practices to monitor student progress and provide timely feedback.

Additional Considerations

1. **Teacher Professional Development:** As education continues to evolve, it is vital to invest in quality professional development for teachers.   In the future, there will be an increased focus on providing educators with opportunities to enhance their pedagogical skills, keep up with the latest research and innovations, and adapt to changing educational contexts.   Professional learning communities, collaborative networks, and mentoring programs will play a crucial role in supporting teacher growth.

2. **Parent and Community Engagement:** The involvement of parents and the wider community is essential for the success of K-12 education.   In the future, fostering strong partnerships between schools, families, and communities will be crucial in supporting student learning and well-being.   Schools should actively engage parents in decision-making processes, provide resources and workshops to support them in their role as partners in education.

3. **Equity and Inclusion:** Promoting equity and inclusion will remain a key focus in the future of K-12 education.   Efforts should be made to address systemic inequalities, create inclusive learning environments, and ensure that all students have access to high-quality education.   This includes providing support for students with diverse learning needs, culturally responsive teaching practices, and eliminating bias and discrimination within educational systems.

In conclusion, the future of K-12 education holds exciting possibilities and significant challenges.   By embracing personalized learning, integrating STEAM education, nurturing cultural responsiveness, and leveraging technology, we can create more equitable and engaging educational experiences for all students. However, bridging the achievement gap, balancing technology integration, preparing students for an uncertain future, redefining assessment, investing in teacher professional development, fostering parent and community engagement, and promoting equity and inclusion will require ongoing commitment and collaboration from all stakeholders.   By working together, we can shape the future of education and ensure that every child has the opportunity to succeed.

Section 2: Higher Education

Subsection 1: Transformative practices in undergraduate teaching and learning

In this subsection, we will explore transformative practices in undergraduate teaching and learning. These practices aim to create a student-centered learning environment that fosters critical thinking, problem-solving skills, and deep engagement with the subject matter. By implementing these practices, educators can empower undergraduate students to become active participants in their own education, leading to improved learning outcomes and increased student satisfaction.

Background

Undergraduate education plays a vital role in shaping students' academic and professional trajectories. It provides students with the foundational knowledge and skills necessary for success in their chosen fields. However, traditional lecture-based teaching methods often fail to engage students or promote deep understanding of the subject matter. Transformative practices in undergraduate teaching and learning seek to overcome these limitations by employing innovative strategies that actively involve students in their own learning process.

Principles of Transformative Practices

Transformative practices in undergraduate teaching and learning are guided by several key principles:

1. **Active Learning:** These practices emphasize active learning strategies that encourage students to participate actively in the learning process, such as collaborative activities, problem-solving exercises, and hands-on experiences. By engaging students in these activities, instructors can enhance their understanding and retention of the material.

2. **Student-Centered Approach:** Transformative practices prioritize the needs and interests of the students. The curriculum is designed to be flexible and responsive to individual learning styles, allowing students to take ownership of their education and tailor their learning experiences to their strengths and interests.

3. **Real-World Relevance:** These practices aim to connect theoretical concepts to real-world applications. By incorporating real-life examples, case studies, and practical projects, instructors can help students see the relevance of their learning

and develop a deeper understanding of how the knowledge can be applied in their future careers.

4. **Critical Thinking and Problem-Solving**: Transformative practices focus on developing students' critical thinking and problem-solving skills. This involves challenging students to analyze complex problems, evaluate evidence, and develop sound arguments. Through this process, students become active participants in constructing knowledge and develop a deeper understanding of the subject matter.

Examples of Transformative Practices

1. **Project-Based Learning**: In project-based learning, students undertake an extended project that requires them to apply their knowledge and skills to real-world problems or scenarios. For example, a biology class may design and execute an experiment to investigate the impact of pollution on local ecosystems. This approach promotes critical thinking, collaboration, and problem-solving skills, as students actively engage in the process of inquiry and knowledge creation.

2. **Flipped Classroom**: The flipped classroom model involves reversing the traditional lecture-based format. Students engage with the content outside of the classroom through pre-recorded lectures or reading materials, which allows for asynchronous learning. In the classroom, the focus shifts to collaborative activities, discussions, and hands-on exercises that deepen students' understanding and application of the concepts. This approach promotes active learning and fosters a more interactive and engaging classroom environment.

3. **Service-Learning**: Service-learning integrates community service with academic instruction. Students apply their knowledge and skills to address real community needs, while also reflecting on their experiences and connecting them to course content. For example, an engineering class may partner with a local organization to design and build a sustainable infrastructure project. This approach promotes civic engagement, leadership skills, and a deeper understanding of social issues.

Resources and Support

Implementing transformative practices in undergraduate teaching and learning requires support and resources for both instructors and students. Institutions can provide professional development and training opportunities for faculty to learn about these practices and incorporate them into their teaching. They can also offer instructional support, such as access to technology and educational resources, to facilitate the implementation of these practices.

Additionally, institutions can create a supportive environment for students by providing academic advising, tutoring, and mentorship programs. These resources can help students navigate the challenges of a student-centered learning environment and ensure their success.

Challenges and Considerations

While transformative practices have the potential to enhance undergraduate teaching and learning, several challenges and considerations need to be addressed:

1. **Resistance to Change:** Transforming teaching practices requires a shift in mindset and pedagogical approaches. Faculty members may be resistant to change, as it can disrupt established routines and require additional effort in course planning and implementation. Effective leadership and institutional support are crucial in motivating and guiding faculty through this transition.

2. **Training and Professional Development:** Faculty may require training and professional development opportunities to effectively implement transformative practices. Institutions should provide ongoing support and resources to help faculty gain the necessary skills and knowledge.

3. **Assessment and Evaluation:** Traditional assessment methods may not adequately capture the learning outcomes associated with transformative practices. Institutions should explore alternative assessment strategies, such as portfolios, group projects, and presentations, that align with the active learning and problem-solving focus of these practices.

4. **Equity and Inclusion:** Institutions need to ensure that transformative practices promote equity and inclusion. Efforts should be made to address the diverse learning needs and backgrounds of students, and to ensure that all students have access to the resources and support necessary to succeed.

Conclusion

Transformative practices in undergraduate teaching and learning have the potential to revolutionize higher education by creating dynamic, interactive, and student-centered learning environments. By adopting these practices, educators can empower undergraduate students to become active participants in their own education, fostering critical thinking, problem-solving skills, and engagement with the subject matter. While challenges exist, institutions can provide the necessary support and resources to facilitate the successful implementation of these practices. Through these efforts, undergraduate education can be transformed, leading to improved learning outcomes and better-prepared graduates for the challenges of the future.

Subsection 2: Success stories in graduate education

Graduate education plays a crucial role in preparing individuals for advanced careers and specialized fields. In this subsection, we will explore some success stories in graduate education, highlighting innovative practices, transformative approaches, and positive outcomes. These success stories demonstrate how graduate education can empower students to excel in their chosen fields and make significant contributions to their respective disciplines.

Success Story 1: Interdisciplinary Research Collaboration

One success story in graduate education involves the implementation of interdisciplinary research collaboration programs. In today's complex and interconnected world, many of the pressing challenges we face require a multidisciplinary approach. Graduate programs that promote collaboration across different academic disciplines can provide students with valuable skills and knowledge that are highly sought after in various industries and research settings.

For example, at XYZ University, a graduate program was established that brought together students from diverse backgrounds such as engineering, biology, and psychology to work on a common research project. This program allowed students to learn from each other's expertise and perspectives, fostering creative problem-solving and innovative solutions.

The interdisciplinary research collaboration not only enhanced students' technical skills but also helped them develop strong communication and team-building abilities. As a result, graduates from this program went on to excel in their respective careers, whether in academia, industry, or entrepreneurship. They were able to tackle complex challenges by drawing upon their interdisciplinary training and effectively collaborating with professionals from different fields.

Success Story 2: Professional Development and Mentorship

Another success story in graduate education revolves around the implementation of comprehensive professional development programs and mentorship initiatives. Graduate students not only need to acquire advanced knowledge in their specific fields but also develop a wide range of transferable skills that are essential for their future professional success.

At ABC University, a graduate program was designed to provide students with immersive professional development experiences. This included workshops on effective communication, project management, leadership, and networking.

Additionally, students were paired with mentors who were established professionals in their fields. These mentors provided guidance, career advice, and support throughout the students' graduate journey.

The professional development programs and mentorship initiatives had a significant impact on students' career trajectories. Graduates from this program reported a higher level of confidence, job satisfaction, and successful career placements. They were well-rounded professionals equipped with not only technical expertise but also the necessary skills to advance in their chosen fields.

Success Story 3: Industry-Academia Collaboration

In recent years, there has been a growing emphasis on fostering collaboration between academia and industry. This collaboration brings together researchers, professionals, and graduate students to work on real-world problems, bridging the gap between theory and practice.

XYZ University successfully implemented an industry-academia collaboration program within its graduate education framework. This program involved partnering with local industries and organizations to provide students with opportunities to engage in applied research projects, internships, and co-op placements.

Through this collaboration, graduate students were able to apply their theoretical knowledge to solve practical problems and gain hands-on experience in their fields. They also had access to industry experts who provided valuable insights and guidance. The program resulted in graduates who were not only well-prepared academically but also had a deep understanding of industry needs and trends.

The success of this industry-academia collaboration program was evident in the high employability rate of graduates. They were highly sought after by employers, who recognized the value of their practical experience and ability to contribute to the industry from day one.

Conclusion

The success stories in graduate education presented above demonstrate the transformative potential of innovative approaches and strategies. Interdisciplinary research collaboration, professional development and mentorship, and industry-academia collaboration can significantly enhance the graduate student experience and prepare students for success in their chosen fields.

To replicate these success stories, it is essential for institutions to invest in interdisciplinary programs, provide comprehensive professional development opportunities, establish robust mentorship programs, and foster collaboration with external stakeholders. By doing so, graduate education can continue to evolve, adapt to emerging trends, and meet the evolving needs of students and employers.

Subsection 3: Integrating Research and Teaching in Higher Education

Integrating research and teaching in higher education is a crucial component of fostering student engagement, promoting innovation, and advancing knowledge in various academic disciplines. This subsection explores the importance of research integration, strategies for incorporating research into teaching practices, and the benefits it brings to both faculty and students.

Importance of Research Integration

Research integration in higher education is essential for creating a dynamic and inquiry-based learning environment. By integrating research into teaching, educators can:

1. Foster critical thinking: Research activities encourage students to analyze and evaluate information critically, promoting independent thinking and problem-solving skills.

2. Cultivate a research mindset: Integrating research helps students develop a mindset that values evidence-based decision-making, creativity, and innovation.

3. Enhance learning outcomes: Research-based teaching strategies have been found to enhance student learning outcomes, deepening their understanding and retention of subject matter.

4. Promote interdisciplinary connections: Research integration encourages interdisciplinary collaboration and the integration of multiple perspectives, fostering holistic learning experiences.

Strategies for Research Integration

To integrate research into teaching effectively, faculty members can employ several strategies:

1. Engage students in authentic research experiences: Design course assignments that require students to conduct original research or contribute to ongoing research projects. This can include data collection, analysis, and interpretation.

2. Incorporate research-based examples and case studies: Use real-world examples and case studies derived from research to illustrate and demonstrate concepts and theories discussed in lectures.

3. Promote research literacy: Teach students how to critically evaluate research papers and enhance their research literacy skills. This includes teaching them how to identify reliable sources, analyze data, and draw evidence-based conclusions.

4. Encourage student-faculty collaborations: Provide opportunities for students to work closely with faculty members on research projects. This can involve mentoring, co-authoring papers, or participating in research conferences.

5. Create research-focused assignments: Assign projects that require students to use research methods, analyze data, and present their findings. This can involve conducting surveys, interviews, experiments, or literature reviews.

Benefits of Research Integration

Integrating research and teaching in higher education offers numerous benefits:

1. Enriched learning experiences: Research integration deepens students' understanding of academic content through active engagement, allowing them to apply theoretical knowledge to real-world situations.

2. Enhanced critical thinking and problem-solving skills: Engaging in research activities encourages students to think critically, analyze data, and solve complex problems, fostering valuable skills needed in their future careers.

3. Increased student motivation and engagement: Research-based learning motivates students by providing opportunities to explore areas of interest, take ownership of their learning, and contribute to the generation of new knowledge.

4. Improved faculty professional development: Engaging in research integration allows faculty members to stay updated with the latest advancements in their field, enhancing their own professional growth and expertise.

5. Advancement of knowledge: By integrating research into teaching, higher education institutions contribute to the advancement of knowledge within their respective disciplines, benefiting both academia and society at large.

Challenges and Solutions

While integrating research into teaching brings many benefits, there are also challenges to consider:

1. Time constraints: Faculty members may face challenges due to limited time available for research activities alongside teaching responsibilities. Addressing this

challenge requires effective time management and institutional support in recognizing the importance of research integration.

2. Access to resources: Accessing research resources, funding, and equipment can be a barrier. Institutions should support faculty members by providing necessary resources and fostering research collaborations.

3. Faculty expertise: Integrating research effectively requires faculty members to have expertise in both research and teaching. Institutions can provide professional development opportunities, mentorship, and support for faculty to enhance their research and teaching skills.

4. Assessment methods: Assessing research-based assignments and projects can be challenging. It is important to develop clear rubrics and assessment criteria that effectively evaluate students' research efforts and outcomes.

5. Bridging research-practice gaps: Integrating research into teaching may require bridging the gap between academic research and real-world applications. This challenge can be addressed by promoting collaborations with industry partners, professional associations, and community organizations.

Examples of Research Integration

Here are a few examples of research integration in higher education:

1. Undergraduate research experiences: Universities can provide research opportunities for undergraduate students through research internships, summer programs, and capstone projects.

2. Community-engaged research: Collaborations between faculty, students, and community organizations can address real-world issues and engage students in impactful research projects.

3. Research-oriented courses: Courses specifically designed to focus on research methods and independent inquiry can provide students with hands-on research experiences.

4. Research centers and institutes: Institutions can establish research centers and institutes to facilitate research collaboration among faculty members, foster interdisciplinary research, and provide resources for research integration.

5. Faculty research-informed teaching: Faculty members can incorporate their own research findings into course content, providing students with the opportunity to learn directly from cutting-edge research in the field.

Resources for Research Integration

Here are some resources that can support research integration in higher education:

1. Faculty development programs: Institutions can offer professional development programs focused on research integration, pedagogy, and inquiry-based teaching methods.

2. Institutional research support: Providing resources, funding opportunities, and access to research databases can empower faculty members to integrate research effectively.

3. Collaborative platforms: Online platforms, such as research networks and collaborative tools, can facilitate research collaboration and knowledge exchange among faculty and students.

4. Research journals and publications: Faculty members can share their research findings in academic journals and publications, promoting the integration of research into teaching materials.

5. Interdisciplinary research centers: Institutions can establish interdisciplinary research centers that promote collaboration across different departments and facilitate research integration.

In conclusion, integrating research and teaching in higher education has numerous benefits for faculty and students alike. By incorporating research activities, faculty members can foster critical thinking, enhance learning outcomes, and promote interdisciplinary connections. Strategies such as engaging students in authentic research, promoting research literacy, and encouraging collaborations can facilitate research integration. While challenges such as time constraints and accessing resources exist, addressing these challenges through institutional support and faculty development can pave the way for successful research integration. Examples and resources further showcase the practical implementation and support available for research integration in higher education. As higher education evolves, integrating research and teaching will continue to play a vital role in fostering innovation, knowledge creation, and student success.

Subsection 5: Innovations in online and blended learning in higher education

In recent years, online and blended learning have gained significant traction in higher education. These innovative approaches to teaching and learning leverage technology to enhance educational experiences and provide flexibility to students. In this subsection, we will explore some of the key innovations in online and blended learning, their benefits and challenges, and their potential impact on higher education.

Online Learning

Online learning refers to educational experiences that take place entirely through digital platforms. It offers a range of benefits, including flexibility in scheduling and location, increased access to courses and resources, and personalized learning experiences. Here are some key innovations in online learning:

1. **Massive Open Online Courses (MOOCs):**   MOOCs are online courses designed to provide open access to high-quality educational content. They offer a variety of subjects and are often provided by prestigious universities and institutions. MOOCs allow learners to access learning materials at their own pace and interact with a global community of learners.   They often incorporate multimedia elements, interactive quizzes, and forums for discussion.

2. **Virtual Reality (VR) and Augmented Reality (AR):**   Virtual and augmented reality technologies have transformed online learning experiences by creating immersive and interactive environments.   With VR, students can participate in virtual labs, explore simulations, and engage in realistic scenarios.   AR enhances learning by overlaying digital information onto the physical world, providing additional context and interactivity. These technologies can be particularly useful in fields such as medicine, engineering, and architecture.

3. **Adaptive Learning Systems:**   Adaptive learning systems use data analytics and artificial intelligence to personalize learning experiences.   These systems collect information about students' performance and tailor the content and pace of instruction to their individual needs.   By adapting to students' strengths and weaknesses, adaptive learning systems can optimize learning outcomes and improve student engagement.

4. **Online Collaborative Tools:**   Online collaborative tools, such as discussion boards, video conferencing platforms, and shared document editors, enable students to engage in collaborative learning experiences. These tools facilitate communication and teamwork, allowing students to collaborate on projects, discuss ideas, and provide feedback to their peers.   Online collaboration can enhance critical thinking, problem-solving skills, and social interaction in an online learning environment.

Blended Learning

Blended learning combines traditional face-to-face instruction with online learning components, providing a more flexible and engaging learning experience. Here are some key innovations in blended learning:

1. Flipped Classroom Model: The flipped classroom model involves delivering instructional content online before the face-to-face class sessions, allowing class time to focus on collaborative activities, discussions, and problem-solving. This model promotes active learning and allows students to engage with the material at their own pace, both individually and in peer groups.

2. Learning Management Systems (LMS): Learning management systems provide a centralized platform for course administration, content delivery, and student interaction. LMS platforms allow instructors to organize course materials, deliver online quizzes and assessments, facilitate discussions, and track student progress. They also enable students to access course materials, submit assignments, and engage in collaborative activities.

3. Gamification: Gamification involves integrating game elements, such as point systems, badges, and leaderboards, into the learning experience. This approach enhances student motivation and engagement by making the learning process more interactive and enjoyable. Gamification in blended learning can be applied to quizzes, assignments, and collaborative activities, encouraging active participation and competition among students.

4. Mobile Learning: Mobile learning leverages the ubiquity of smartphones and tablets to provide learning experiences anytime and anywhere. With mobile learning, students can access course materials, engage in discussions, and complete assignments using their mobile devices. The flexibility and convenience of mobile learning facilitate continuous learning and support students with busy schedules.

Innovations in online and blended learning have the potential to transform higher education by expanding access to quality education, promoting active learning, and enhancing student engagement. However, these innovations also bring some challenges, including the need for robust technical infrastructure, faculty training in online pedagogy, and ensuring equitable access for all students. As higher education continues to evolve, harnessing the power of online and blended learning will be crucial for the future of education.

Example: An example of the successful implementation of online and blended learning in higher education is the Khan Academy. Founded in 2008, the Khan Academy is a non-profit organization that offers online courses and resources across various subjects. With its extensive library of videos, practice exercises, and personalized learning tools, the Khan Academy has revolutionized the way students learn and teachers teach. Its adaptive learning system allows students to learn at their own pace, while the gamified elements, such as earning badges and leveling up, keep students motivated and engaged. The Khan Academy's success has inspired many similar online platforms and has become a go-to resource for students of all ages around the world.

Resources: - Massive Open Online Courses (MOOCs): `https://www.classcentral.com/report/how-to-choose-a-mooc-platform/` - Virtual Reality in Education: `https://er.educause.edu/blogs/2019/4/whats-next-for-virtual-reality-in-education` - Khan Academy: `https://www.khanacademy.org/`

Discussion Questions: 1. What are the advantages and disadvantages of MOOCs as a form of online learning? 2. How can virtual reality and augmented reality enhance the learning experience in higher education? 3. How can instructors effectively integrate gamification into blended learning environments? 4. What are the potential ethical considerations and risks associated with online learning? 5. How can institutions ensure equal access to online and blended learning opportunities for all students, regardless of their backgrounds or resources?

Exercises: 1. Choose a subject of your interest and explore available MOOCs. Compare different MOOC platforms in terms of course offerings, instructor quality, and user reviews. 2. Design a virtual reality experience for a specific educational purpose, such as training medical students or teaching architectural principles. 3. Create a gamified activity for a blended learning environment, incorporating game elements to enhance student engagement and motivation. 4. Conduct research on the impact of online learning on student outcomes. Analyze the results and discuss any limitations or implications of the study. 5. Develop a plan to implement a blended learning model in a higher education institution. Consider the necessary resources, training requirements, and potential challenges.

Section 3: Vocational and Adult Education

Subsection 1: Effective Strategies for Vocational Education and Training

Vocational education and training (VET) plays a crucial role in preparing individuals for specific occupations and equipping them with the practical skills required to succeed in the workforce. This subsection will explore some of the effective strategies that can enhance the quality of VET programs and improve outcomes for learners.

Understanding the Importance of Vocational Education and Training

Vocational education and training offers a pathway for individuals to acquire the knowledge, skills, and competencies necessary for specific occupations. It focuses on hands-on learning and practical application of skills, providing learners with relevant and marketable qualifications. Effective VET programs can address the needs of industries, support economic growth, reduce unemployment, and foster social inclusiveness.

Industry Engagement and Partnerships

For VET programs to be effective, strong partnerships between education providers and industry stakeholders are essential. These partnerships ensure that the training offered aligns with industry needs and current employment trends. Industry representatives can contribute to curriculum development, provide work placements and apprenticeship opportunities, and offer insights into emerging technologies and practices. This collaboration facilitates the development of industry-relevant skills and enhances the employability of VET graduates.

Work-Based Learning

Work-based learning is a key component of vocational education and training. It provides learners with valuable real-world experiences and allows them to apply their knowledge and skills in authentic work settings. Work-based learning can take various forms, such as apprenticeships, internships, on-the-job training, and simulated workplace environments.

One effective strategy is the integration of work-based learning into the curriculum, combining classroom instruction with hands-on practice. This approach allows learners to develop technical skills, gain industry-specific knowledge, and develop a professional work ethic. Employers can also play an active role in mentoring and assessing learners during work-based learning experiences, providing valuable feedback and guidance.

Flexible and Customized Training Pathways

Recognizing the diverse needs and backgrounds of learners, VET programs should offer flexible and customized training pathways. This approach allows individuals to tailor their learning to their specific goals, interests, and learning styles. Flexible training pathways can include options for part-time and online learning, recognition of prior learning, and modularized courses that allow learners to acquire skills incrementally.

Customized training pathways can also cater to the needs of specific industries or occupations. For example, programs can be designed in collaboration with industry stakeholders to address skills shortages in high-demand sectors. By offering personalized training options, VET programs can better meet the needs of learners and provide them with relevant and timely skills.

Technology Integration

Integrating technology into VET programs can enhance learning experiences and prepare learners for the digital workplace. Technology tools and resources can support skill development, enable interactive learning activities, and provide access to up-to-date industry information. Virtual simulations, online collaboration platforms, and mobile learning apps are examples of technological resources that can be incorporated into VET programs.

Additionally, technology can facilitate distance learning and bring learning opportunities to individuals who may have limited access to traditional training settings. Online courses and virtual classrooms can provide flexibility and convenience, enabling learners to engage in VET programs remotely.

Quality Assurance and Evaluation

To ensure the effectiveness of VET programs, quality assurance and evaluation mechanisms are crucial. Regular assessment and review of program outcomes, learner achievement, and industry relevance can help identify areas for improvement and inform future program development.

Quality assurance processes can involve external validation, where industry experts evaluate the program against industry standards and benchmarks. Learner feedback and surveys can also provide valuable insights into the strengths and weaknesses of the program.   By continuously reviewing and refining their programs, VET providers can ensure that they are delivering high-quality training that meets the needs of learners and industry.

Challenges and Recommendations

While effective strategies can enhance vocational education and training, several challenges need to be addressed.   These challenges include outdated training content, limited access to work-based learning opportunities, and the need for continuous professional development for VET trainers. Additionally, equity and inclusivity should be prioritized to ensure that individuals from disadvantaged backgrounds have equal access to quality VET programs.

To overcome these challenges, it is recommended that VET providers regularly engage with industry stakeholders to ensure program relevance. Collaboration with employers and community organizations can also expand work-based learning opportunities for learners.   Moreover, investments in professional development for VET trainers and the integration of inclusive practices can promote equitable access and success for all learners.

Conclusion

Effective vocational education and training strategies involve industry engagement, work-based learning, flexible training pathways, technology integration, quality assurance, and addressing challenges through collaboration and continuous improvement. By implementing these strategies, VET programs can effectively prepare individuals for the workforce, contribute to economic growth, and meet the evolving needs of industries and learners.

Subsection 2: Adult Learning Success Stories and Practical Strategies

In this subsection, we will explore some inspiring success stories and practical strategies in adult learning. Adult education plays a vital role in empowering individuals to enhance their skills, pursue new careers, and achieve personal and professional growth. We will examine real-world examples and discuss effective strategies that can be implemented in various adult learning contexts.

Success Story: Lifelong Learning for Professional Development

Mary is a middle-aged professional who has been working in the marketing industry for several years. She wants to enhance her skills and stay updated with the latest trends in digital marketing. Instead of pursuing a traditional degree program, Mary decides to explore online courses and workshops that offer flexible learning options.

Mary comes across an online platform that provides a wide range of digital marketing courses, taught by industry experts. She enrolls in a course that focuses on search engine optimization (SEO) and social media marketing. The course curriculum is designed to address the specific needs and challenges faced by professionals in the marketing industry.

Throughout the course, Mary engages in practical exercises, case studies, and discussions with fellow learners. She receives personalized feedback from the instructor, which helps her refine her skills and apply them to real-world scenarios. At the end of the course, Mary successfully completes a project that demonstrates her understanding of SEO and social media marketing strategies.

This success story highlights the effectiveness of lifelong learning opportunities for professionals. Online platforms and flexible learning options enable adults to acquire new skills and knowledge that are directly applicable to their careers. The personalized feedback and practical exercises ensure that learners can immediately apply what they have learned in their professional settings.

Strategy: Collaborative Learning Communities

Collaborative learning communities are effective strategies for promoting engagement and knowledge sharing among adult learners. In these communities, individuals with similar interests or goals come together to learn from each other, share resources, and collaborate on projects.

One example of a collaborative learning community is a professional learning network (PLN). A PLN is a group of professionals who connect and communicate through online platforms, social media, or regular meetups. They share articles, resources, and insights related to their field of interest, stimulating discussions and fostering a culture of continuous learning.

For instance, a group of educators interested in implementing project-based learning may form a PLN where they exchange ideas, share successful project examples, and support each other in overcoming challenges. They may organize online webinars or offline workshops to deepen their understanding of project-based learning.

By actively participating in a collaborative learning community, adult learners can expand their professional networks, gain diverse perspectives, and access a wealth of knowledge and resources. These communities provide ongoing support and opportunities for growth, ensuring that adult learners can continue to learn and develop throughout their lives.

Strategy: Prior Learning Assessment

Adult learners often bring valuable knowledge and experiences from their personal and professional lives. Recognizing and assessing their prior learning is a crucial strategy to ensure that their previous knowledge is acknowledged and integrated into their educational journey.

Prior learning assessment (PLA) involves evaluating and granting credit for skills and knowledge acquired through work experience, informal learning, or other non-traditional learning experiences. This process allows adult learners to receive recognition for what they already know, saving them time and effort in completing a degree or certification program.

In one example, a working professional named John has been working as a software developer for over a decade. He decides to pursue a degree in computer science to advance his career. However, instead of starting from scratch, John takes advantage of the PLA process offered by his chosen university.

Through a portfolio assessment and an interview, John is able to demonstrate his proficiency in various programming languages, software development methodologies, and problem-solving skills. As a result, he receives credits for several courses and is able to skip introductory programming and database courses.

PLA not only recognizes adult learners' prior knowledge but also motivates them by providing a clear pathway to achieve their educational goals. It allows adult learners to focus on filling gaps in their knowledge and acquiring new skills that complement their existing expertise.

Additional Resources

1. *The Power of Lifelong Learning: Adult Education and Training in a Changing Society* by Tom Schuller - This book explores the importance of adult education in today's rapidly changing world and provides insights into effective strategies for lifelong learning.

2. *The Adult Learner: The Definitive Classic in Adult Education and Human Resource Development* by Malcolm S. Knowles - This seminal work examines the

unique characteristics of adult learners and offers practical tips for designing effective learning environments for them.

3. *The Handbook of Adult and Continuing Education* edited by Arthur L. Wilson, et al. - This comprehensive handbook covers a wide range of topics related to adult education, including program design, instructional strategies, assessment, and research methods.

4. Online platforms such as Coursera, Udemy, and LinkedIn Learning offer a vast array of online courses and micro-credentials that cater to the diverse learning needs of adult learners.

Remember, adult learning is a dynamic field, and these success stories and strategies are just a glimpse of the possibilities. By staying open to innovation and embracing the unique needs of adult learners, educators and institutions can empower adults to achieve their educational goals and thrive in the modern workforce.

Subsection 3: Bridging the Gap between Education and Workforce Demands

One of the key challenges in education today is the need to bridge the gap between what is taught in schools and the skills demanded by the workforce. As technology and the global economy continue to evolve, there is a growing disconnect between traditional educational models and the skills required for success in the modern workplace. In this section, we will explore strategies and approaches for addressing this gap, ensuring that education prepares individuals for the demands of the workforce.

Understanding the Workforce Demands

Before we can bridge the gap between education and workforce demands, it is crucial to have a clear understanding of what skills and competencies are needed. The modern workplace requires not only academic knowledge but also a range of technical, interpersonal, and problem-solving skills.

One way to gain insight into specific workforce demands is to engage with industry professionals and employers. Conducting surveys, interviews, and focus groups with representatives from different sectors can help identify the skills that are in high demand and the areas where existing educational programs fall short.

For example, in the field of technology, employers often express a need for individuals who are well-versed in coding languages, data analysis, and cybersecurity. In the healthcare sector, there is a growing demand for professionals with expertise in telemedicine, health informatics, and patient-centered care. By understanding these specific demands, educational institutions can tailor their curriculum and learning experiences to meet the needs of the workforce.

Integrating Workforce Skills into the Curriculum

Once the specific workforce demands are identified, the next step is to integrate the relevant skills and competencies into the curriculum. This can be achieved through a combination of curriculum redesign, the inclusion of specialized courses or modules, and the incorporation of real-world applications and experiences.

One effective approach is to establish partnerships between educational institutions and industry stakeholders. By collaborating with local businesses and organizations, schools can gain access to industry expertise and ensure that their curriculum reflects the current trends and requirements. These partnerships can also provide students with opportunities for internships, apprenticeships, and mentorship programs, bridging the gap between education and practical work experience.

It is also essential to incorporate hands-on, project-based learning opportunities that simulate real-world scenarios. For example, in a vocational education program, students can work on projects that mirror the tasks they would encounter in the workplace, such as developing marketing campaigns, creating business plans, or designing prototypes. By engaging in these types of activities, students can develop essential skills such as critical thinking, problem-solving, collaboration, and communication.

Promoting Career Guidance and Exploration

Another vital aspect of bridging the gap between education and workforce demands is providing students with robust career guidance and exploration opportunities. Many students enter the education system without a clear understanding of the diverse career paths available to them. By providing comprehensive career counseling and exploration programs, educational institutions can help students make informed choices about their educational pathways.

This can be achieved through career fairs, guest speaker events, and mentorship programs, where students can interact with professionals from different industries and gain insights into various career options. Additionally, schools can collaborate with local businesses to offer job shadowing programs or internships, allowing students to get a firsthand experience of the workplace and develop a better understanding of their career interests and aspirations.

Furthermore, it is essential to equip students with career readiness skills, such as resume building, interview preparation, and networking skills. These skills not only enhance their employability but also empower them to navigate the job market successfully.

Addressing Challenges and Ensuring Relevance

Bridging the gap between education and workforce demands is not without its challenges. One common challenge is the rapid pace of technological advancements, which can quickly make certain skills obsolete. To address this, educational institutions must prioritize adaptability and continuous learning. By fostering a culture of lifelong learning, individuals can acquire new skills and stay relevant in the face of evolving workforce demands.

Another challenge is the limited resources and funding available for educational programs. To overcome this, schools can leverage partnerships with community organizations, businesses, and government agencies to secure funding for initiatives that address the skills gap. Additionally, schools can explore alternative funding models, such as grants, sponsorships, and scholarships, to support programs that bridge the gap between education and workforce demands.

In conclusion, bridging the gap between education and workforce demands is crucial for ensuring that students are adequately prepared for the modern job market. By understanding the specific workforce demands, integrating relevant skills into the curriculum, providing career guidance and exploration opportunities, and addressing challenges, educational institutions can play a pivotal role in preparing individuals for success in the workforce. Through collaborative efforts between educators, industry stakeholders, and policymakers, we can create an educational system that meets the needs of learners and empowers them to thrive in the ever-changing world of work.

Key Takeaways:

+ Understanding specific workforce demands is essential for bridging the gap between education and the job market.

+ Integration of relevant skills into the curriculum through partnerships with industry stakeholders and hands-on, project-based learning.

+ Providing robust career guidance and exploration opportunities for students to make informed career choices.

◆ Adapting to challenges such as technological advancements and limited resources through a culture of lifelong learning and strategic partnerships.

Subsection 4: Promoting lifelong learning and re-skilling in the workplace

Promoting lifelong learning and re-skilling in the workplace is crucial in today's ever-evolving job market. The rapid advancements in technology and changes in industries require individuals to continuously update their skills and knowledge to remain competitive and adaptable. This subsection explores the importance of lifelong learning, strategies for promoting it in the workplace, and the benefits it brings for both employees and organizations.

The Importance of Lifelong Learning

Lifelong learning refers to the ongoing process of acquiring new knowledge, skills, and attitudes throughout one's life. It involves a proactive approach to personal development and empowers individuals to stay relevant and adaptable in a rapidly changing world.

In the modern workplace, lifelong learning is essential for several reasons. Firstly, it enables employees to acquire new skills that are in demand, allowing them to take on new roles and responsibilities within their organizations. It also equips individuals with the tools to navigate technological advancements, ensuring they can leverage new technologies effectively.

Furthermore, lifelong learning enhances employability. As industries evolve, certain job roles become obsolete while new ones emerge. Employees who actively engage in continuous learning are better equipped to transition into new roles or industries, safeguarding their careers against unemployment or stagnation.

From an organizational standpoint, promoting lifelong learning cultivates a culture of innovation and growth. Organizations that invest in learning and development initiatives create a motivated and engaged workforce that is willing to take on new challenges and contribute fresh ideas. Additionally, by fostering a learning culture, organizations can attract and retain top talent, as employees value opportunities for growth and development.

Strategies for promoting lifelong learning

Promoting lifelong learning requires a strategic approach that integrates learning and development initiatives into the workplace. Here are some effective strategies to consider:

1. Provide Learning Opportunities: Offer a range of learning opportunities, such as workshops, seminars, webinars, conferences, and online courses, to cater to different learning preferences and schedules. Encourage employees to take advantage of these opportunities and allocate dedicated time for learning activities.

2. Support Self-directed Learning: Encourage employees to take ownership of their learning journey by providing access to online learning resources, e-learning platforms, and digital libraries. Foster a supportive environment where employees feel empowered to seek out and pursue learning experiences that align with their career goals.

3. Establish Mentoring Programs: Pair experienced employees with less experienced ones to facilitate knowledge transfer and skill development. Mentoring programs provide valuable learning opportunities and support the growth and development of employees.

4. Encourage Continuous Feedback: Establish a feedback culture that encourages regular performance discussions and constructive feedback. This feedback can help identify areas for improvement and guide employees towards appropriate learning opportunities.

5. Recognize and Reward Learning Achievements: Acknowledge and reward employees who actively engage in lifelong learning. This can be through certifications, promotions, or even simple recognition in team meetings. By celebrating learning achievements, organizations reinforce the value placed on continuous learning.

Benefits of Lifelong Learning for Employees and Organizations

Promoting lifelong learning in the workplace yields numerous benefits for both employees and organizations.

For employees, lifelong learning leads to personal and professional growth. It enables individuals to stay relevant in their field, adapt to new technologies, and expand their skill set. Lifelong learners are more likely to progress in their careers, secure promotions, and enjoy increased job satisfaction.

Furthermore, lifelong learning enhances employability, providing individuals with the flexibility to explore new career paths. Employees who continually update their skills and knowledge are better prepared to navigate job market fluctuations and secure employment in high-demand industries.

For organizations, lifelong learning contributes to increased productivity and innovation. Employees who engage in continuous learning bring fresh perspectives, creative problem-solving abilities, and up-to-date knowledge to the workplace. This culture of innovation can lead to increased efficiency, improved products or services, and enhanced competitiveness.

Moreover, organizations that invest in learning and development initiatives demonstrate a commitment to employee growth and well-being. This fosters a positive work environment, boosts employee morale, and aids in the retention of top talent.

Caveats and Challenges

While promoting lifelong learning in the workplace brings numerous benefits, there are some caveats and challenges to consider.

One challenge is resistance to change. Some employees may be resistant to learning new skills or technologies due to fear of the unknown or complacency. Overcoming this resistance requires effective change management strategies, clear communication, and showcasing the benefits of lifelong learning.

Another challenge lies in the availability of resources. Companies must provide employees with access to learning opportunities, whether through financial support for courses or by allocating dedicated time for learning activities. Adequate resources and support are essential for promoting lifelong learning effectively.

Additionally, measuring the impact of lifelong learning initiatives can be challenging. It is important to establish clear learning objectives and evaluate the outcomes of learning activities to ensure they align with organizational goals. Implementing feedback mechanisms and assessment tools can help gauge the effectiveness of these initiatives.

Real-world Example: Upskilling Programs in the Tech Industry

The tech industry is a prime example of an industry that prioritizes lifelong learning and upskilling. With technology evolving at a rapid pace, professionals in the tech industry must continually update their skills to remain relevant.

Many tech companies offer upskilling programs to their employees. For instance, Google has a program called "Google Skills Academy" that provides employees with opportunities to learn new skills and technologies through both internal and external training programs. By investing in the learning and development of their workforce, Google ensures that its employees have the necessary skills to thrive in a dynamic industry.

Another example is Microsoft's "Microsoft Learn" platform, which offers a wide range of free online courses and resources for individuals to learn Microsoft technologies. This platform empowers employees, as well as external learners, to enhance their skills and stay updated with the latest industry trends.

These examples showcase how tech companies are actively promoting lifelong learning and re-skilling to stay competitive and foster a culture of continuous growth and innovation.

Conclusion

Promoting lifelong learning and re-skilling in the workplace is essential in a rapidly evolving job market. By emphasizing continuous learning, organizations and employees can adapt to changing technological landscapes, enhance skills, and stay competitive. Through effective strategies, organizations can create a culture of learning, leading to increased productivity, innovation, and employee satisfaction. Lifelong learning is not just a personal responsibility but a collective effort that benefits individuals and organizations alike, driving success in the modern workplace.

Further Reading

1. Smith, M., & Smith, E. (2019). Lifelong Learning in the Digital Age: Sustainable for All in a Changing World. UNESCO. 2. Davies, D. et al. (2017). Continuing Professional Development in Higher Education: Global Perspectives. Routledge. 3. Hase, S., & Kenyon, C. (2000). From Andragogy to Heutagogy. Ulti-BASE In-Site. 4. Carey, S. (2014). The End of College: Creating the Future of Learning and the University of Everywhere. Penguin Random House. 5. Siemens, G., & Long, P. (2011). Penetrating the Fog: Analytics in Learning and Education. EDUCAUSE Review.

Subsection 5: Challenges and opportunities in vocational and adult education

Vocational and adult education play a crucial role in preparing individuals for the workforce and supporting lifelong learning. However, like any educational system, there are both challenges and opportunities that need to be addressed in order to ensure the success of vocational and adult education programs. In this section, we will explore some of the key challenges and opportunities in this field and discuss potential strategies for overcoming them.

Challenges in vocational and adult education

1. **Lack of awareness and misconceptions:** One of the main challenges is the lack of awareness and misconceptions about vocational and adult education. Many individuals still perceive these fields as being less prestigious or less valuable than traditional academic pathways. This can lead to a stigma around vocational and adult education, affecting the enrollment and participation of students in these programs.

2. **Limited funding and resources:** Vocational and adult education programs often face financial constraints and limited resources. This can result in outdated equipment, inadequate infrastructure, and a lack of qualified teachers and trainers. Insufficient funding can also limit the development and implementation of innovative teaching methodologies and technologies.

3. **Changing job market:** The rapid advancements in technology and automation are rapidly changing the job market. This poses a challenge for vocational and adult education providers in designing and delivering programs that align with the evolving demands of industries. It is critical for these programs to stay updated and connected with industry trends to equip learners with the necessary skills for the workforce.

4. **Engaging adult learners:** Adult learners have unique needs and motivations compared to traditional students. Balancing work, family, and other commitments can make it challenging for them to dedicate time and energy to education. Adult learners often require flexible learning options that accommodate their busy schedules and personalized support that caters to their individual needs.

5. **Lack of career pathways and recognition:** Vocational and adult education programs should provide clear career pathways and opportunities for learners. However, in some cases, there is a lack of well-defined pathways or recognized qualifications for certain vocational fields. This can lead to limited job prospects or a lack of recognition for the skills acquired through vocational programs.

Opportunities in vocational and adult education

1. **Meeting industry demands:** Vocational and adult education programs can seize the opportunity to work closely with industries and employers to understand their needs and develop curricula and training programs accordingly. By aligning with the demands of the job market, these programs can ensure that learners acquire skills that are relevant and in demand.

2. **Integration of technology:** Technology can play a transformative role in vocational and adult education. Online learning platforms, virtual reality

simulations, and interactive learning tools can enhance the learning experience and provide opportunities for hands-on practice. Embracing technology can also help overcome limitations in resources and increase access to education for remote or underserved populations.

3. **Recognition of prior learning:** Recognizing and valuing the skills and knowledge that adult learners bring from their prior experiences can empower and motivate them to engage in further education and career advancement. Accreditation systems that acknowledge prior learning can provide opportunities for adults to gain formal recognition for their existing skills and abilities.

4. **Collaboration and partnerships:** Collaboration between vocational and adult education providers, employers, industry associations, and community organizations can create a supportive ecosystem for learners. Partnerships can facilitate work-integrated learning, apprenticeships, internships, or other opportunities that bridge the gap between education and industry, enhancing learners' employability.

5. **Promoting lifelong learning:** Vocational and adult education programs can foster a culture of lifelong learning by encouraging individuals to continuously update their skills and knowledge. Offering flexible learning options, such as part-time or evening classes, and providing ongoing professional development opportunities can support adults in their career progression and adaptability in a changing job market.

Case study: Bridging the skills gap in the healthcare sector

The healthcare sector faces a significant skills gap due to the rapid advancement of medical technologies and increased demand for healthcare services. A successful vocational and adult education initiative in this sector is the development of specialized training programs for medical technicians, such as radiology technicians or medical coders.

These programs address the challenge of limited resources by using state-of-the-art simulators and virtual learning environments to provide hands-on training. They also collaborate closely with healthcare institutions to ensure that the curriculum aligns with industry needs and includes real-world problem-solving experiences.

Furthermore, these programs recognize the prior learning of adult learners by offering accelerated pathways for individuals with relevant experience or certification in related fields. Recognizing prior learning accelerates the training process and ensures that learners can quickly enter the workforce with a formal qualification.

To promote ongoing professional development and lifelong learning, these programs offer continuing education opportunities for healthcare professionals. This allows them to keep pace with advancements in the field and remain competitive in the job market.

By addressing these challenges and capitalizing on these opportunities, vocational and adult education programs can play a vital role in bridging the skills gap in the healthcare sector and other industries.

Conclusion

Vocational and adult education face unique challenges, such as misconceptions, limited resources, changing job markets, engaging adult learners, and the lack of clear pathways. However, there are also significant opportunities, including meeting industry demands, integrating technology, recognizing prior learning, collaboration and partnerships, and promoting lifelong learning.

By addressing these challenges and embracing these opportunities, vocational and adult education can effectively prepare individuals for the workforce, support career advancement, and contribute to the overall development of society. It is crucial for policymakers, educators, and industry leaders to work together to create an enabling environment for vocational and adult education to thrive.

Index